Footprints of the
Painter and Scott Families
of Missouri

Minuteman illustration courtesy of the Smithsonian Institution Research Information System: Stephens, Ann S. *Pictorial History of the War for the Union*. New York: Benjamin W. Hitchcock, 1866. Public Domain.

Published by
Compass Flower Press

Compass
Flower
Press

Columbia, Missouri
compassflowerpress.com

Library of Congress Control Number: 2022923359

ISBN: 978-1-951960-45-2

Footprints
of the
Painter and
Scott Families
of
Missouri

Virgil E. and Emma Jo Painter Raines

Compass Flower Press
Columbia, Missouri

Table of Contents

About the Authors vii

Dedication ix

Preface 1

Chapter 1 Introduction 3

Chapter 2 Those Boxes.. 7

      Painter Pedigree Chart.. 8

      Scott Pedigree Chart.. 9

Chapter 3 First Generation...11

Chapter 4 Second Generation 15

      Dilts Family Photo 14

Chapter 5 Third Generation 19

Chapter 6 Fourth Generation... 27

      Murphy Family Photo... 43

Chapter 7 Fifth Generation 47

Chapter 8 Sixth Generation 69

Chapter 9 Seventh Generation 93

Chapter 10 Eighth Generation 103

Chapter 11 Ninth Generation 109

Chapter 12 Hawkins Cemetery 113

Chapter 13 Final Footprints 115

Acknowledgments 117

About the Authors

Colonel (U.S. Army Retired) Virgil E. "Sonny" Raines Jr. was born in Jackson County, Missouri, to V. Elwood Raines and Ruby Nadine Adams Raines. He was raised on a farm in Shelby County, Missouri, attended school there, and graduated from Paris High School in Paris. He worked in the defense industry for three years and married Emma Jo Painter in August 1963. He enlisted in the army and obtained a commission as a second lieutenant. He became an army aviator, served in several overseas assignments, and commanded from captain to colonel level during his nearly thirty-year career.

Virgil Raines graduated from Park University and the University of Pennsylvania with multiple degrees, and is also a graduate of the Army Command and General Staff College and the Army War College.

He served on several college faculties and as a professor of military science at the Naval War College. He has published articles on the war on drugs, several technical articles on military aviation, and a book, *Horse Sense—William Rains and the Missouri Seventh Volunteer Cavalry*. Soon to be published is his book *Beat Your Drum Loudly: The Raines–Painter Revolutionary War Patriots.* He also published several short articles on family members who were killed in the Second World War. Virgil is a member of the Sons of the American Revolution and teaches genealogy research to potential DAR and SAR members as well as to patients at veterans' hospitals.

Emma Jo Painter Raines was born in Monroe County, Missouri, to Oliver and Leta Blanche Scott Painter, attended school there, and graduated from Paris High School. She graduated from Gem City College and worked in the defense industry until her husband's military service began.

Jo has worked as a Department of the Army civilian and as an accountant. She served in her chapter of the Daughters of the American Revolution as chapter regent and as registrar for several years. She made and donated dozens of "Quilts of Valor" to service veterans in both Missouri and Texas.

The Raineses live on a farm in Boone County, Missouri, and have three children and seven grandchildren.

Dedication

I met Gordon Richard Scott in 1963 shortly after Emma Jo and I were married. He lived in Kansas City and we in St. Louis. He just stopped by. We hit it off well, but our careers and lives quickly took different directions, and my exposure to Richard and his soon-to-be family was infrequent. We were busy men with family responsibilities, but I always seemed to know what he was up to as a college administrator and family man. He was a high-performance man, and what he did was worthy of note. I held him in high regard.

Richard's untimely passing in 2002 led to some of his personal records being passed on to Jo (Emma Jo). We took note, but did not quickly delve into them. I began research on the Patriots *book five years ago and had met a research roadblock with the Scott family line. I remembered that Richard's records consisted primarily of family research he had accomplished about forty years ago. He had done a lot of work. I soon discovered he pursued his research much as I do—intensively! We would have made good detective partners. He met the same roadblocks as I but never gave up. I quickly found his work with the Murphy and Crook family lines, which we found very helpful. In the instance of the Crook family line, we merely followed the hints provided by a professional researcher he had collaborated with to quickly push our knowledge of that line back four generations. Thanks Richard!*

I am confident Richard would be most intrigued with the stories we have developed and new family groups we have discovered. He has been a part of the story, and we want to recognize his contributions to our research even though we are way too late in doing so. We offer him a tip of the hat and often enjoy the end of the day thinking of him. Richard, this one's for you!

Preface

In some historical cultures, family history was passed down through word of mouth over many generations. Few cultures follow that tradition now. I remember my parents revealing tidbits about our family history when I was much younger. They seemed to know who all my ancestors were and where they lived. I know now their knowledge, although considerable, was very limited. I grew up in a community where it seemed as though I was kin to more people than not. It seemed everyone not only knew who I was, but knew my parents and a lot about my ancestors. I thought that was normal. Things have changed.

This fast-moving society has resulted in families being more geographically separated, which greatly reduces interaction between children, young adults, adults, and the elderly. I see young people who have little knowledge of their grandparents, let alone older ancestors several generations in the past. That is not their fault. It is clearly the challenge for the senior generations to gather and pass this information and the lessons contained within to future generations. It is not the responsibility of familysearch.org, ancestry.com, or some unknown contributor to a popular genealogy website. Pearl S. Buck said it best:

> The lack of emotional security of our American young people is due, I believe, to their isolation from the larger family unit. No two people – no mere father and mother – as I have often said, are enough to provide emotional security for a child. He needs to feel himself one in a world of kinfolk, persons of a variety in age and temperament, and yet allied to himself by an indissoluble bond which he cannot beak if he could, for nature has welded him into it before he was born.

This project and the resulting book is an effort by Emma Jo and myself to begin fulfilling our responsibility.

Chapter 1
Introduction

"Why waste your money looking up your family tree? Just go into politics and let your opponents do it for you."

—Mark Twain

This project begins with Emma Jo Painter Raines, who is the daughter of Oliver Forest Painter and Leta Blanche Scott of Paris, Missouri. The family is presented by generation by family lines contained within that generation—Oliver and Leta Blanche Painter representing generation one, going back in time by generation. The Painter line will be presented first, followed by the Scott line within each generation. As we travel back in time, the tree grows each generation, actually doubling. The Pedigree Charts in the following chapter will be useful in seeing the various relationships and names. One can imagine that by the time we travel back five or six generations, there will be many family lines to explore and discuss, hence the importance of these graphics.

Each successive family group will be presented with known information, such as birth, death, marriages, and children, as well as where they lived and any pertinent stories we have discovered. It is our intent to present each family line back in time to arrival on the shores of the United States, with a synopsis of the family origins in Europe, if known.

You will see the following family lines presented:

Painter Lines:

Dilts	Greening	Webb
Boren	Hawkins	Schultz
Baker	Whitledge	Greenwood
Rownd	Smith	Tandy
Carman	Johnston	Allendar
Stribling	Seibert	

Scott Lines:

Murphy	Allen	Shulse
Simon	Myers	Whitledge
Crooks	Ashby	Burris
Roney	Oglesby	Abney
Embree	Witt	Schneider
Duncan	Isaacs	

We consider this material a companion to our forthcoming book, *Beat Your Drum Loudly*, a record of Revolutionary War Patriots of the Raines/Painter family line. We reveal the stories of forty-three Patriots from which the Raines/Painter lines descended. There are actually over one hundred Patriots documented in this book when the fathers and brothers of these Patriots are included. We will not repeat those stories, but this book will be an interesting accompaniment to this project. Nineteen of the forty-three Patriots are direct ancestors in the Painter/Scott lines.

As one can imagine, there will be gaps and unknowns in the history of these family groups. We continue our efforts to find missing ancestors and enrich and add to the family history. We simply have not included a name of an ancestor in this book unless we have proven that relationship. In some instances, we use the "preponderance of evidence" logic, but we will reveal that caveat when appropriate. For privacy reasons, we include the name of only one individual still living. While the focus will be on direct ancestors, grandparents, great-, great-great, etc. we believe it important to tell the stories of aunts and uncles and their relationships, as this information greatly enriches these complex family stories. Again, the Pedigree Charts following this chapter will be useful in the true perspective of the stories and assist in keeping everything straight.

The Painter-Scott Lines

The Painter family can claim residence in Missouri for more than 190 years. George Washington Painter moved to Florida, Missouri, in the mid-1830s from West Virginia. The family immigrated from Germany prior to the Revolutionary War and lived in Pennsylvania, then Virginia/West Virginia and then Missouri. The German version of the name is "Bender." In a German dialect it would have been pronounced sounding like Painter, thus the change. It was probably not Americanized, as some European names, just mispronounced and spelled as it sounded.

We are uncertain of the full American history of the Scott line. We ran into what we in the genealogy field call a "brick wall" beyond the fourth generation. Work continues in that regard. It's probably Scotch, and we are confident we will find a Revolutionary War Patriot in that line as Davis Scott, grandfather of Cerra Gorda Scott, was a remarkable man—educated, sophisticated, and daring. He was an early pioneer of both Howard and Monroe counties. We believe we will someday complete this story. We do know that the Scotts have been in Missouri since late 1817, well over two hundred years.

This is an appropriate place to discuss the spelling of names and places. We may not have it all right. The spelling of first names is worthy of discussion. We often found the spelling of given names varied with time for a given person. In some instances, if a person could not read or write, they were at the mercy of whomever did the paperwork. Even if someone was literate, correct spelling was often not that important, as long as documents could be read easily and understood. Read the unpublished expedition journals and notes of Meriwether Lewis and you will see my point. We found important documents, such as marriage and death records, using varied spellings for a person's given name. We make notes on our finds throughout the book. The spelling of family names sometimes varies over time for various reasons. I found during the writing of the *Patriots* book that one family name had twenty-three variations of spelling. That is, I found records of twenty-three different spellings for the name Reinhart. There are actually more if you consider the Prussian/German spellings. To sum it up, do not subject the spellings of given and family names in this book to today's standards for spelling. We attempted to spell them like we saw them. It may not be a typo, but merely a part of history!

The use of middle names was not common with colonial Americans, except for more prominent families. We found few middle names used on important documents. Perhaps a person had a middle name, but it might have been omitted from those documents and thus lost to history. We included middle names of family members if we could document their use. We found middle names of both men and women to be very useful in research, as middle names were often the family names of a person's mother. Not proof of relationship, but useful.

Chapter 2
Those Boxes

"If you cannot get rid of the family skeleton, you might as well make it dance."

—George Bernard Shaw

The complexity of discussing more than 256 family groups, their children, brothers, and sisters over seven or eight generations has given us the challenge of helping readers keep in mind where each family group fits in the family tree as they read the stories. The following two Pedigree Charts hopefully do that. They are organized from generation one, with Oliver Painter and Leta Blanche Scott presented as generation one. These charts show six generations for both family lines. You will later see that we portray more than six generations, and in a few instances, seven or eight later in the book. Six generations were enough for these charts. Way too many boxes.

It is easy to recognize where the trail runs out on these charts and our research. In most cases of "unknown" entries, we have an idea of the names for that generation, but we were unable to prove the connection with solid genealogical evidence. That work continues. In one line, we have no idea beyond the fourth generation—the Scotts.

Painter Pedigree Chart

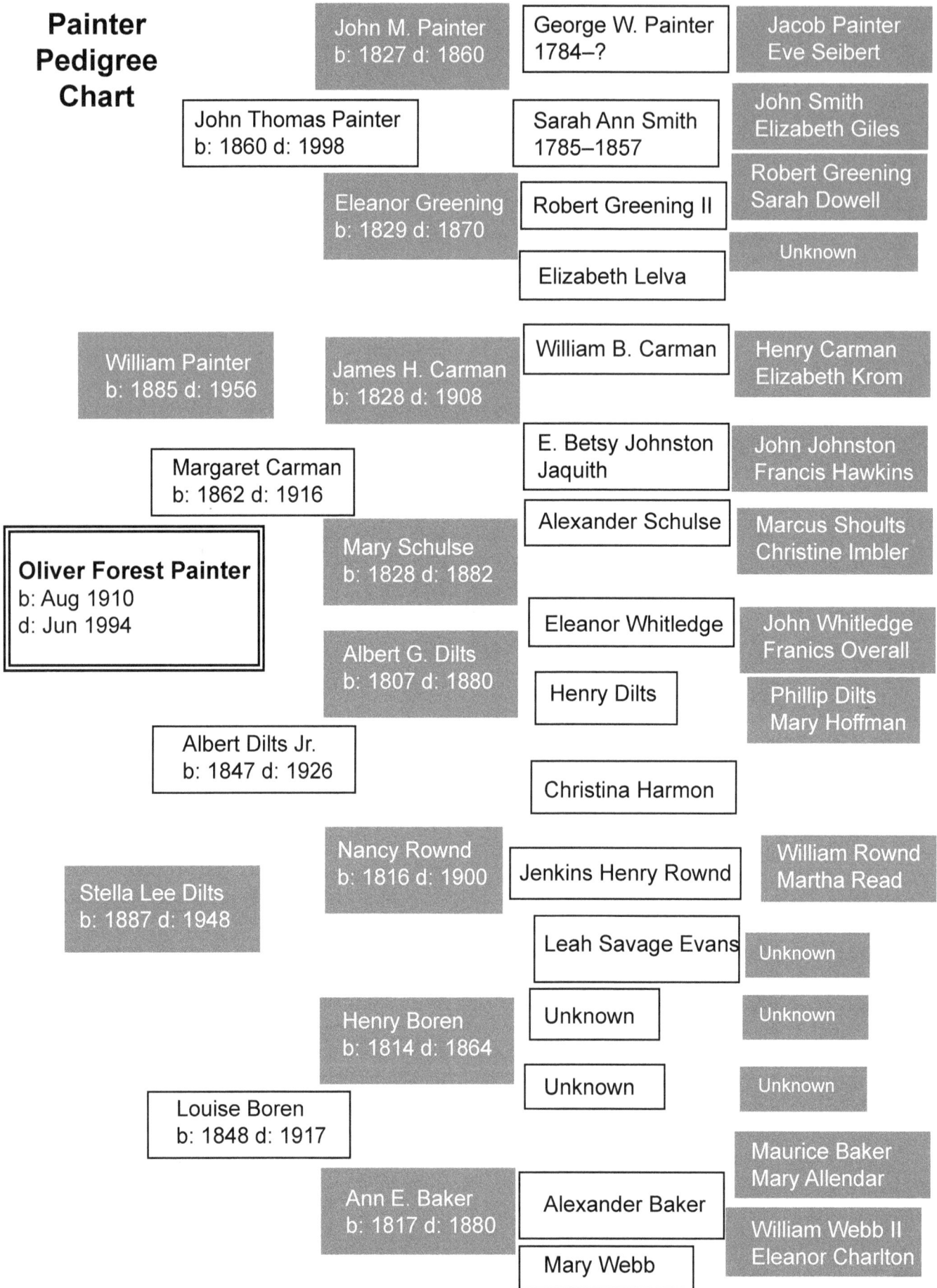

John Thomas Painter
b: 1860 d: 1998

John M. Painter
b: 1827 d: 1860

- George W. Painter 1784–?
  - Jacob Painter
  - Eve Seibert
- Sarah Ann Smith 1785–1857
  - John Smith
  - Elizabeth Giles

Eleanor Greening
b: 1829 d: 1870

- Robert Greening II
  - Robert Greening
  - Sarah Dowell
- Elizabeth Lelva
  - Unknown

William Painter
b: 1885 d: 1956

James H. Carman
b: 1828 d: 1908

- William B. Carman
  - Henry Carman
  - Elizabeth Krom
- E. Betsy Johnston Jaquith
  - John Johnston
  - Francis Hawkins

Margaret Carman
b: 1862 d: 1916

Mary Schulse
b: 1828 d: 1882

- Alexander Schulse
  - Marcus Shoults
  - Christine Imbler
- Eleanor Whitledge
  - John Whitledge
  - Franics Overall

Oliver Forest Painter
b: Aug 1910
d: Jun 1994

Albert G. Dilts
b: 1807 d: 1880

- Henry Dilts
  - Phillip Dilts
  - Mary Hoffman
- Christina Harmon

Albert Dilts Jr.
b: 1847 d: 1926

Nancy Rownd
b: 1816 d: 1900

- Jenkins Henry Rownd
  - William Rownd
  - Martha Read
- Leah Savage Evans
  - Unknown

Stella Lee Dilts
b: 1887 d: 1948

Henry Boren
b: 1814 d: 1864

- Unknown
  - Unknown
- Unknown
  - Unknown

Louise Boren
b: 1848 d: 1917

Ann E. Baker
b: 1817 d: 1880

- Alexander Baker
  - Maurice Baker
  - Mary Allendar
- Mary Webb
  - William Webb II
  - Eleanor Charlton

Scott Pedigree Chart

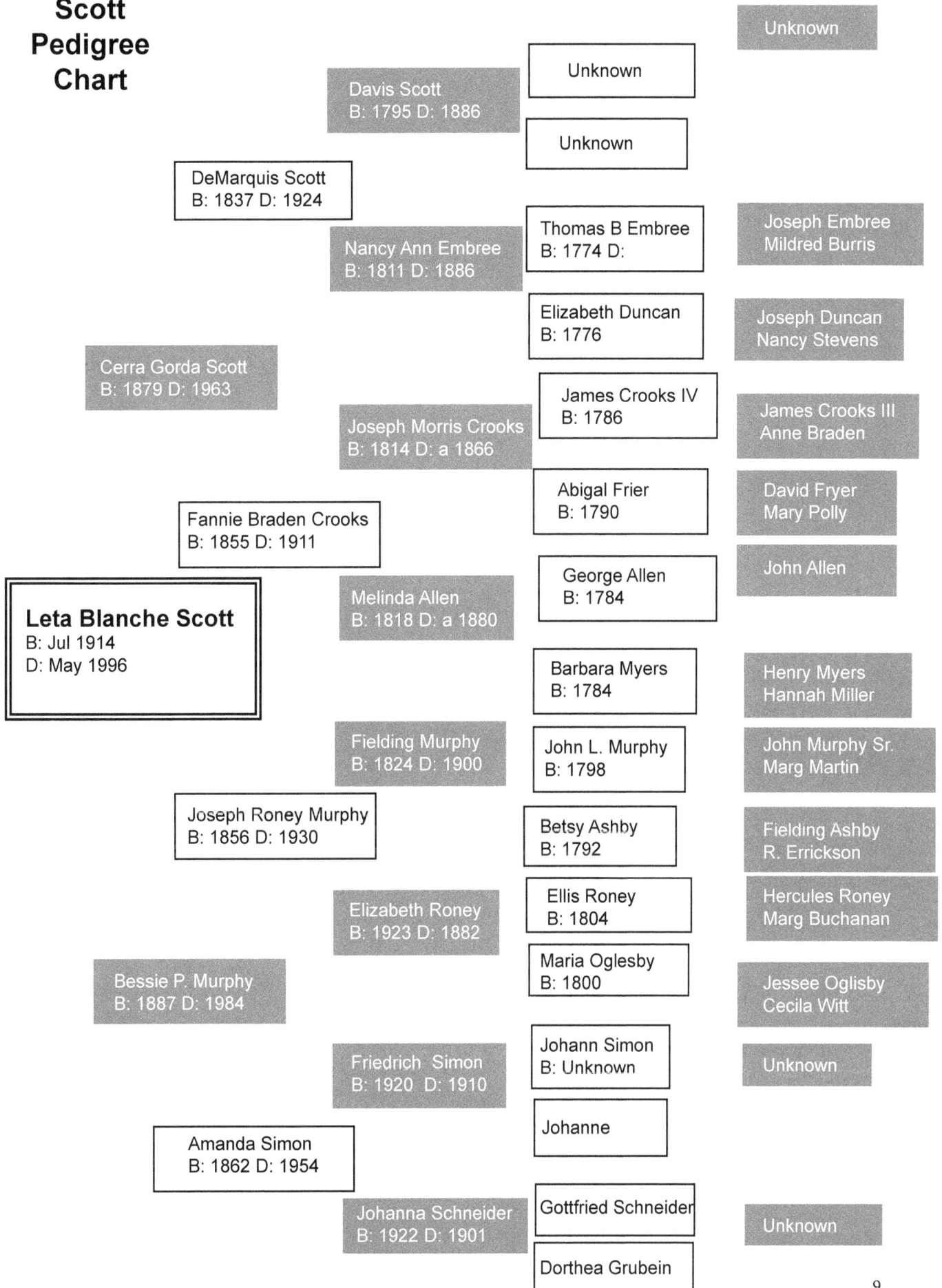

- **Leta Blanche Scott**
  B: Jul 1914
  D: May 1996
  - Cerra Gorda Scott
    B: 1879 D: 1963
    - DeMarquis Scott
      B: 1837 D: 1924
      - Davis Scott
        B: 1795 D: 1886
        - Unknown
          - Unknown
        - Unknown
      - Nancy Ann Embree
        B: 1811 D: 1886
        - Thomas B Embree
          B: 1774 D:
          - Joseph Embree
            Mildred Burris
        - Elizabeth Duncan
          B: 1776
          - Joseph Duncan
            Nancy Stevens
    - Fannie Braden Crooks
      B: 1855 D: 1911
      - Joseph Morris Crooks
        B: 1814 D: a 1866
        - James Crooks IV
          B: 1786
          - James Crooks III
            Anne Braden
        - Abigal Frier
          B: 1790
          - David Fryer
            Mary Polly
      - Melinda Allen
        B: 1818 D: a 1880
        - George Allen
          B: 1784
          - John Allen
        - Barbara Myers
          B: 1784
          - Henry Myers
            Hannah Miller
  - Bessie P. Murphy
    B: 1887 D: 1984
    - Joseph Roney Murphy
      B: 1856 D: 1930
      - Fielding Murphy
        B: 1824 D: 1900
        - John L. Murphy
          B: 1798
          - John Murphy Sr.
            Marg Martin
        - Betsy Ashby
          B: 1792
          - Fielding Ashby
            R. Errickson
      - Elizabeth Roney
        B: 1923 D: 1882
        - Ellis Roney
          B: 1804
          - Hercules Roney
            Marg Buchanan
        - Maria Oglesby
          B: 1800
          - Jessee Oglisby
            Cecila Witt
    - Amanda Simon
      B: 1862 D: 1954
      - Friedrich Simon
        B: 1920 D: 1910
        - Johann Simon
          B: Unknown
          - Unknown
        - Johanne
      - Johanna Schneider
        B: 1922 D: 1901
        - Gottfried Schneider
          - Unknown
        - Dorthea Grubein

9

Chapter 3
First Generation

"Get your facts first, then you can distort them as you please."

—Mark Twain

Oliver Forest Painter

Born: 9 August 1910, Monroe County, Missouri
Died: 23 June 1994, Paris, Missouri
Married: 1 May 1935, Monroe County, Missouri
Buried: Walnut Grove Cemetery, Paris, Missouri

Oliver was the first son of William Franklin and Stella Lee Dilts. His father was a farmer living east of Paris four to five miles and north of what is now State Route U. He attended Kirkland Grade School near his home and graduated from Paris High School in 1929. He boarded in Paris while attending school there. He had one brother, Clifton Lloyd, born in 1915. He also had a younger sister, Grace Bee, who died in infancy. Oliver has said she is buried in Hawkins Cemetery in an unmarked grave.

He told many stories of his youth, but we regrettably did not record all of them. Times were tough in his youth. He told of hopping a freight train that contained coal cars, throwing the coal off piece by piece until they reached Paris, then walking home with a burlap sack gathering the bounty. He attended high school and worked odd jobs for support. Some of those jobs involved learning mechanical skills from some well-known local tinkerers, the Curtright brothers of Paris. Those skills served him well the remainder of his life. Fishing and hunting were not only a source of recreation for him and his family, but probably an important source of food. He was good at both and enjoyed these sports his entire life.

In notes provided by him, he gave his birth place as being located on a farm rented by his father in Section 34 of Jefferson Township east of Paris and north of County Road U, or the old Paris to Florida road. The intersection of Route U and the gravel road leading to that farm is near the Pleasant View Church. (The church no longer stands.) His notes relate his family made several moves in his time at home. His father bought mother Maggie Carman Painter's home in 1915, and they lived there for a year or two. That home was east on Route U. We believe Maggie had sold the farm land associated with that home, so Frank continued to rent farmland.

After graduation, he worked in the Paris area. We remember him telling of working on construction of State Highway 24 from Moberly to Monroe City. He married Leta Blanche Scott on 1 May 1935 in Paris, Missouri by Reverend Willard Reavis. We have a copy of that license with witness names. This was a depression-era economy. We believe he supported himself and his new wife by mechanic work with the Curtright brothers' garage. When World War II began, he quickly discovered that he could not pass an armed forces physical. He had flat feet. His two brothers-in-law, Raymond and Jr. Scott, were quickly drafted. He filled their shoes working on the Scott farm during the war. He told me stories of transporting friends to and from Fort Leonard Wood, Missouri, as they entered and left the armed forces during the war. The farm was located on Middle Fork Salt River and fishing was an important form of recreation and source of food for the entire family. He and Leta Blanche eventually purchased land on the south side of the river near the Scott family farm. That land is still in our possession.

Following the war and the return of the Scott brothers from their military duty, Oliver began carpenter work, sometimes in partnership with Mac, Aubrie, and Emmett Donavan of Holiday, Missouri. He used a portion of Bill Robinson's lumber yard as a shop in Paris. He built several houses in the Monroe County area and did general carpentry repair work. He was extremely good at finish carpenter work. He did not hurry and lived by the adage of "measure twice and cut once." Materials were expensive, and he wasted nothing. It did not take a lot of tools to be a general carpenter, and he transported them in the trunk of his car. He had them all and took great care of them. I still have some of those tools in my possession. They still work quite well.

I remember after Jo and I married in 1963, we would visit Paris on weekends and usually stay with Oliver and Leta Blanche. It was in 1965 when he started construction of their new house in Paris. Much of the framing for that house came from old homes he tore down for the lumber. On one occasion, I helped him tear down an old barn east of Paris to recycle that lumber. There was an old wood box full of rusty tools left after the large barn was down. He told me to get that box. I did not know him that well at that point, and I did not jump right on the task of claiming that old dirty box. He told me again in pretty direct terms to get that box. I got that box and took it home. It sat in our stack of stuff that you never quite know what to do with for several years until I examined it and the contents in 1972. I found that it was made of walnut boards twenty-six inches wide. Beautiful lumber. The tools were old, and I still have them in a box somewhere, but that box sets in a prominent location at my feet today, reclaimed, refinished, and looking great fifty-seven years later—one of our prized possessions.

He did carpenter work until a few years prior to retirement, when he went to work for the Paris school district. He worked there until the mid-1970s and retired. He built a wood shop behind his house. This was a gathering place for wannabe woodworkers who would seek his advice on various woodworking projects. I learned much from him there.

Oliver and and Leta Blanche had two children: Emma Jo, mentioned earlier, and Danny Ray, who was born in 1945. Danny graduated from Paris High School and did construction work as long as he could work. He served in the Army National Guard during the Vietnam War. Danny never married and died in 2008. He is buried in Walnut Grove Cemetery in Paris.

Virgil E. and Emma Jo Painter Raines

Leta Blanche Scott
Born: 24 July 1914, Monroe County, Missouri
Died: 11 May 1996, Paris, Missouri
Buried: Walnut Grove Cemetery, Paris, Missouri

Leta was the third child of Cera Gorda and Bessie Pauline Murphy of rural Monroe County, Missouri. She had three brothers and two sisters:
- Joe Mark 1911–2002
- Anna Frances Reaves 1913–1986
- Lois Amanda Dowell 1916–2005
- Cera Gorda Jr. 1917–2010
- Raymond Edward 1919–1985

She grew up on the Scott farm east of Paris and attended one-room schools in that neighborhood until she attended high school in Paris, graduating in 1932. Her family home was located near Middle Fork Salt River and was of original board-clad log construction. It had been added on to over the years and took on the appearance of a great two-story home. It was historically significant and was torn down by the University of Nebraska after the land was purchased by the Corps of Engineers for construction of Mark Twain Lake. It was built by early French settlers in Missouri well prior to Missouri becoming a state and well prior to the War of 1812.

Her brother Joe Mark lived in Kansas City, Missouri, most of his working life and owned a home on State Line Boulevard for many years. He was a member of the Masonic lodge and a Boy Scout Eagle. He married Elsie Foster of Kansas City, and they had two children.

Her sister Anna Frances Reavis lived her entire life in the Paris, Missouri, area and married Willard Reavis. They had no children.

Her sister Lois Amanda Dowell lived in Monroe and Audrain Counties her entire life. She married John William (J.W.) Dowell, and they had three children.

Her brother Cera Gorda Jr. served in the army in World War II in the Pacific theater and was wounded. I believe he was in the infantry. He returned to the family farm. He married Nadine Bradley of Moberly, and they had three sons. In later years they moved to LaGrange, Missouri.

Her youngest brother, Raymond, also served in the army during World War II in the infantry in the European theater. After the war, he returned to the farm and farmed there until the land was sold to the Corps of Engineers. He never married.

Back Row: Frank Painter, Stella "Tillie" Painter, Frank Burdett, Dora "Dode" Dilts Burdette, Albert P.Dilts, Sarah "Sadie" Pearl Ralston Dilts, Grover Bare, Lucretia "Creat" Dilts Bare

Middle Row: Mary Dilts, (Celeste on lap) Jack Dilts, (Lester on lap), Thula Painter, Isaac William Painter, A. G. Dilts, (Nell Painter on lap-William's daughter) Louisa Boren Dilts, Minerva "Minnie" Dilts Scobee, Ely Scobee

Kneeling: Paul Scobee, Herbert Painter (William's son), Mary Painter (seated on rug), Oliver Painter (seated on rug), Rolston Dilts (A.P.'s son), Agnes Scobee, Helen Dilts, Dora Lee Painter

Chapter 4
Second Generation—Grandparents

Definition of mythology: Genealogy without documentation
−Author unknown

William Franklin Painter
Born: 15 August 1885, Florida, Monroe County, Missouri
Died: 1 January 1956, Paris, Monroe County, Missouri
Married: 25 November 1907, Stoutsville, Monroe County, Missouri
Buried: Pleasant Hill Cemetery, Paris, Monroe County, Missouri

William (Frank), father of Oliver F. Painter above, was the son of John T. (Thomas) Painter and Margaret Lee "Maggie" Carman of Florida, Missouri. He was born on the Painter farm very near Florida. He had six brothers and sisters. Their stories will be told later in this book.

Frank married Stella Lee Dilts in Stoutsville, Missouri, on 25 November 1907. They were married in the home of Stella's sister Minnie Scobee, who is pictured in the following photo. Their oldest child, Grace Bee, was born in 1907 and died in 1908. She is buried in Hawkins Cemetery. They also had two sons, Oliver and Clifton Lloyd (1916–1962). Clifton married Bettie L. Hatton on 12 September 1942. They had several children, and some of their descendants still live in Missouri.

The family photo shown, dated around 1913, contains two generations of Painters and three generations of the Dilts family, and they are all identified. Isaac William Painter—in the second row, seated—is the son of Robert Parker Painter, a half-brother of Frank's father, so he is a half-cousin. See the Isaac William mystery in the following chapter.

Frank farmed in Monroe County east of Paris for his entire life until retirement when he moved to Paris, Missouri. He is buried in Pleasant Hill Cemetery east of Paris with Stella in a well-marked grave.

Oliver related an story about Frank and Stella's unfortunate farm-buying experience in 1929. They were in the process of probate settlement of her father A.G. Dilts's estate. There were expecting to inherit about $80,000 from his estate, which was deposited in the Stoutsville Bank. He was in the process of buying a farm and obtained a temporary loan from a private financier until the estate was finally settled. He deposited the borrowed money in the same bank, which quickly closed its doors due to the stock market crash. He lost the borrowed money plus the inheritance. He never bought the farm.

Stella Lee Dilts Wife of Franklin Painter
Born: 11 February 1887, Monroe County, Missouri
Died: 8 March 1948
Married: 25 November 1907
Buried: Pleasant Hill Cemetery, Monroe County, Missouri

Stella was the daughter of Albert G. Dilts and Louise B. Boren of Ralls County, Missouri. Albert was a farmer owning a farm near Palmyra, Missouri. Stella had five brothers and sisters who will be discussed later. Stella is also buried in Pleasant Hill Cemetery.

The Painter-Dilts Family
Circa: 1913

Cerra Gorda Scott
Born: 4 December 1879, Paris, Monroe County, Missouri
Died: 15 September 1963, Paris, Monroe County, Missouri
Married: 25 August 1910, Paris, Monroe County, Missouri
Buried: Paris, Missouri, Walnut Grove Cemetery

"Gordie" was the son of DeMarquis Scott and Fannie Braden Crooks of Paris, Missouri. DeMarquis was a farmer east of Paris his entire life. Gordie had two sisters, Mary and Anna Lenore. Mary died in infancy and Anna (1878–1970) married Harvey Leonard Carter (1873–1908), and they had two children. Anna was a minister, and she and husband Harvey are buried in Pleasant Hill Cemetery near her father and mother's grave sites.

Gorda and Bessie Pauline Murphy married in Monroe County on 25 August 1910. They had six children: Joe Mark, Anna Frances, Leta Blanche, Lois Amanda, Cerra Gorda Jr., and Raymond Edward, all discussed above.

We have an early family photo of the Scotts taken circa 1920. We have many later photos of small groups and individuals, but this is a striking photo.

Gorda was a graduate of Gem City College of Quincy, Illinois, the same college from which his granddaughter Emma Jo graduated. He was a farmer his entire life, owning a farm on the banks of Middle Fork Salt River. That farm was purchased by the Army Corps of Engineers to clear land for construction of Mark Twain Lake shortly after his death. He also owned the "Murphy farm" for several years before selling it to his son Jr. Scott.

The home of Cerra and Bessie was an historical home, being one of the first three homes in Jackson Township of Monroe County. It was part of the original "Smith Settlement" established soon after Missouri gained statehood in 1821. The Scott house was referred to as the Matthew Mappin home, built sometime after the land was bought from the land office in 1828. The house was not of log construction but made of heavy cut timbers with clapboards being attached to the exterior. It was built with the second-story balcony overlooking Middle Fork Salt River. The home was featured in an article in the

Monroe County Appeal shortly after the Corps of Engineers purchased the home for lake construction. The home was probably eligible for listing with the National Historical Homes register and was slated for movement to the University of Omaha for preservation, but local pressure prevented it from being moved out of state. It was torn down and burned rather than being moved out of state. The Scotts played no role in the fate of the house.

The Smith Settlement was not quite as old as the Ezra Fox settlement of the Middle Grove area but was established shortly after the Ezra Fox and Embree families settled there. We will discuss the Fox/Embree settlement later in this book, as that settlement is connected to the Painter-Scott family history also. While the Cerra Scott home might not have been the oldest home in Monroe County, it was among the oldest. Emma Jo can claim to have been born in one of the oldest homes in the county and certainly the oldest home in Jackson Township.

We have the dissertation of Karen Hunt, in which she surveyed the homestead and located the original farm buildings associated with that homestead. We have worked with Karen on historical digs in Monroe County.

Bessie Pauline Murphy
Born: 26 March 1887
Died: 10 May 1984
Married: 25 August 1910
Buried: Paris, Missouri, Walnut Grove Cemetery

Bessie was the daughter of Joseph Roney Murphy and Anna Maria Amanda Simon of Paris, Missouri. The Murphys were Monroe County farmers owning land very near the Scott farm discussed above. Bessie had four brothers and sisters to be discussed later. She was the mother of six children and ten grandchildren. Bessie and Gorda were married fifty-three years before his death in 1963.

Chapter 5
Third Generation—Great-Grandparents

"When a society or civilization perishes, one condition can always be found. They forgot where they came from."

—*Carl Sandburg*

John Thomas Painter
Born: 13 June 1860
Died: 20 March 1898, in Missouri
Married: 18 May 1880, Monroe County, Missouri
Buried: Probably in Hawkins Cemetery

Thomas was the son of John M. "Amos" Painter and Eleanor Greening of Florida, Missouri. His father was married twice, first to Narcissa Stribling (1830–1855) and then to Eleanor. We will speculate that he was named after the husband of his father's sister Elizabeth (1817–1853), who died young after giving birth to several children who also died young. Their story follows later in this book. His uncle's name was John Thomas.

Some facets of Thomas's life were slow to surface. What we have found is the product of normal genealogy records research that yielded less than a complete life story of his and his wife Maggie's short lives. These records were subsequently enriched by notes provided by Oliver Painter many years ago that we only recently rediscovered. The story remains incomplete, but enough has been found to provide an interesting but sad story.

Thomas was born on his family farm near Florida, Missouri. His father had previously been married, with two children from the first marriage. He was the third of four children from his father's second marriage. This was a family of farmers and landowners, so Thomas followed in their footsteps. His father, John Amos, died a few months after the birth of John Thomas at the age of thirty-three.

Thomas married Margaret Lee "Maggie" Carman of Monroe County on 18 May 1880 in Monroe County. We have their marriage license. He soon purchased a farm about one and a half miles west of Florida on the south side of what is now State Route U that connects Florida with Paris. That land is now located on the southwest corner of State Route 107 and Route U. He had a mortgage on the farm and soon constructed a house on the land. The location can be seen on the 1898 Monroe County atlas. This land is now owned by the U.S. Army Corps of Engineers and is adjacent to Mark Twain Lake at a highly visible location at that road junction. No homes remain on that land, and it is in view of Mark Twain Lake.

For years we believed our knowledge of their children was complete, as it was based on census reports of 1880 soon after their marriage and the 1900 census two years after the death of Thomas. We knew of three children. One died young at age twenty-one, and two, including Jo's grandfather, lived much longer lives. That was what consisted of our knowledge of that family group for years.

A few years ago, we obtained the probate records from their estate, dated a few months after the death of Thomas. Maggie accounted for five children at home, two of which we were unaware of. She gave their names but not ages. We quickly reviewed the 1900 and 1910 census report with Maggie as head of household. It listed the three known children, but buried in the questions posed by the census, Maggie revealed seven children born, with four still alive. We then again reviewed the notes provided by Oliver Painter and found where he accounted for a child that died of TB at the age of thirteen. His name was Mason. Oliver's notes mentioned another son. That gave us the seven children. Problem solved: we had their names!

Actually, our search had merely begun and will not quickly be solved, as two of the names of sons were identical with names of cousins all living within a few miles of each other and nearly the same age. We found it extremely difficult to distinguish between these sons. At one point, we speculated that uncle Robert Parker Painter and great-uncle George Oliver Painter had taken two of their sons to raise, but that was not supported by facts. They had sons with the same names, but they were clearly different people. As a matter of note, uncle Robert Parker Painter's farm was located just across the road from John and Maggie's home. Here is what we know of John Thomas and Maggie Carman's seven children:

Isaac (N. or W.) Painter. Listed in the probate records. Never shown on a census report of the family. He was not mentioned in Oliver Painter's notes. His half-uncle Robert Parker had a son with the same name and possibly born within two years of this Isaac. They were close neighbors and we know the life of one of them quite well. One married Darthula Dilts, sister of Stella Dilts, who was Jo's grandmother and wife of William Frank Painter. We have records giving this Isaac's birth date as 1778, two years before the marriage of John Thomas and Maggie, so he is probably not their son. The Isaac that married Darthula is buried in Walnut Grove Cemetery with her and died in 1952. Most existing family records state he is the son of George Parker Painter, not John Thomas. We located death records of an Isaac William Painter that died in the Fulton State Hospital in 1952 and was buried in the new Perry, Missouri, cemetery by a Perry undertaker's name given with his father's name of George Parker Painter. This was probably the son of George Parker Painter who was buried in Paris, not Perry. So where is Isaac William Painter, son of John Thomas and Maggie Painter? He was listed on the 1898 probate records, but not present for the 1900 census. We do not know his birth date, but he was likely old enough to strike out on his own by 1900, but again, we have never found any records of his life in Missouri or anywhere else. He could not be one of the four remaining living children accounted for by Maggie in the 1900 and 1910 census, as we know who they were. He may have died of TB between 1898 and 1900 and may be buried in Hawkins Cemetery. He remains a mystery.

Mason Painter. Name given in the Oliver Painter notes. Not listed on the 1900 or 1910 census of Maggie or on any Missouri census or probate records. Oliver stated he died of TB at about thirteen years of age. He likely died before 1898 because Maggie did not list him in the probate records. He was likely born after 1880 and died prior to 1898. Oliver stated he was likely buried in Hawkins Cemetery without a stone. Remember, the 1890 census was destroyed, so it is of no help in this instance.

William Franklin Painter. Jo's (Emma Jo's) grandfather, born in 1885 and died in 1956. His story is told above.

Fred Painter. Listed in the probate records. Never shown on any census pertaining to Thomas or Maggie. Uncle George Oliver Painter had a son named William Frederick, born within one year of our estimated birth year for this Fred. Not the same men. We find no records for a second Fred or Fredrick Painter ever in Monroe County. Maybe he died or left home between the 1898 probate court proceedings and the 1900 census. If he left home, he went far, as we find no records in Missouri for him. Furthermore, he could not be one of the four living children accounted for by Maggie in census reports. Could he have died of TB between 1898 and 1900?

Mary Elizabeth "Lizzie" Painter (1889–1911). Lizzie is shown in the probate records and the 1900 and 1910 census as living in the household of Maggie. She died in 1911 of TB and is buried in Hawkins Cemetery without a headstone according to Oliver Painter and her death certificate. She never married.

Jessie Irene Painter (1895–1941). Listed in the probate records and 1900 census as living with Maggie. She was married by 1910 to Earl Wolverton, who lived very near her mother's farm. She eventually moved to Iowa, had three children, and was buried in Lucas County, Iowa. We have more of her records but will not recount them in this book, but her story is also a sad story.

Marcus Newton Painter. Name and general information provided about his life by Oliver Painter in his notes. Newton was probably the oldest of their children. He is not shown in any census report in the home of John Thomas and Maggie and is not shown in the probate records of 1898. He likely did not live in the household then, and was married by 1900. He was born 21 Feb 1881, and died: 1 March 1940 in Sand Springs, near Tulsa, Oklahoma. He married Lucy Lyon in 1900, in Florida, Missouri and they had one child, Elbert Ross. He farmed in Monroe County until he and Lucy divorced after 1910 in Hannibal, Missouri where he had become a union barber. He lived in Hannibal during World War I and worked as a barber. He registered for the draft but was not drafted. After he and Lucy divorced following the war, he moved to Oklahoma, remarried, and lived the remainder of his life there. He is buried in Sand Springs, Oklahoma.

Emma Jo recalls a story told by her father, Oliver, in which his father, Frank, and his mother, Stella, along with Oliver and his brother Clifton, moved to Oklahoma, probably near his uncle Marcus Newton, around 1920. They were at that location for only a short time, and their intertest in Oklahoma quickly dried up and they returned to Monroe County.

Thomas farmed on his farm until sometime after the birth of his daughter Jessie Irene in 1895. According to Oliver's notes, he caught TB and moved to Red Lodge, Montana, pursuing a more favorable climate to fight the deadly disease. We first assumed he died in Red Lodge, but we now believe he returned home prior to his death. We probably misunderstood Oliver's statement and assumed incorrectly. He probably died in Monroe County and likely is buried in Hawkins Cemetery, just a mile or so down current Route U from his home. There is no headstone for his grave.

TB devastated this family. We believe only three of the of nine persons in this family survived to live normal lives. They were Marcus Newton, William Franklin and Jesse Irene. Of course Margaret "Maggie" lived to about age fifty-three, her life was not easy and was certainly shortened by this disease.

Margaret Lee "Maggie" Carman Wife of John Thomas Painter
Born: 4 May 1862, Monroe County, Missouri
Died: 8 March 1916, Indian Creek Township, Monroe County, Missouri
Married: 18 May 1880 and again in 1915
Buried: Hawkins Cemetery

Maggie was the daughter of James Henry B. Carman and Mary Ann Schultz of Marion County, Missouri. She was one of ten children. A matter of note is that her sister Mary Jane married Robert Parker Painter, half-brother of John Thomas above. Robert Parker was the first son of John Amos Painter and his first wife Narcissa Stribling. Maggie was the great-granddaughter of Henry Carman, Revolutionary War Patriot to be discussed later in this book. Remember that Robert Parker Painter and wife Mary Jane lived across the road from Maggie.

After the death of John Thomas in 1898, Maggie remained on the farm of about 150 acres. She eventually sold most of the land except for the house, which she sold to son William Franklin in 1915. Her daughter Lizzie remained in her household until her death in 1911. Lizzie is buried in the Hawkins Cemetery in an unmarked grave. We believe that Maggie's sons Isaac, Mason, and Fred are also buried there based on statements made by Oliver. Her mother and father are buried there also in well-marked graves.

Maggie married Thomas Tandy Donaldson of Indian Creek Township near Stoutsville in 1915. Thomas's first wife had died in 1908. We are uncertain of her marriage date, but she did not live long after her marriage. She died in March 1916 at the age of fifty-three and is buried in Hawkins Cemetery. Her grave is also unmarked, and her death certificate reflects her burial in Harmony Cemetery, which was the original name of Hawkins Cemetery. We have copies of that land transfer. The old Harmony Baptist Church was demolished when the Corps of Engineers purchased the land. The church never owned the cemetery.

Thomas Donaldson's middle name of Tandy caught our attention. His father, Robert, married Minerva Stribling, daughter of Tandy Stribling. Tandy was also the father of Narcissa, who was the first wife of John Amos Painter, father of John Thomas Painter. Without question, Maggie knew the Donaldson family, as her first husband was a descendant of that family and they lived within maybe five miles of each other. They were not married long.

Albert G. Dilts Jr.
Born: July 1847, Mississippi
Died: 29 March 1926, Quincy, Illinois
Married: 1870 to Louise B. Boren
Buried: Walnut Grove Cemetery, Paris, Missouri

Albert was the son of Albert G. Dilts and Nancy Rownd of Marion County, Missouri. He married Louise B. Boren in 1870 in Marion County. Albert and Louise had eight children:
- Albert Pendleton 1870–1941
- Minerva Virginia "Minnie" Scobee 1871–1928
- George H. 1879–1950
- Darthula "Thula" Painter 1881–1954. She married Isaac Painter, son of Robert Parker Painter discussed above.
- Centinental "Cennie" 1883–unknown. Killed by a horse and buried in the Scobee Cemetery and was later relocated to the Walnut Grove cemetery in Paris, Missouri.Lucretia "Crete" Bare 1884–1951
- Stella Lee 1887–1948. Married Frank Painter.
- Dora "Dori" Burditt 1890–1969

Albert, Louise, and children Albert P., Darthula, Lucretia, and Stella are shown in the Painter-Dilts photo shown on page 14.

Albert was a farmer owning a farm first in Marion County, then in neighboring Ralls County by 1890, and later in neighboring Monroe County. He died in a hospital in Quincy, Illinois, in 1926 and was buried in Scobee Cemetery, which was later relocated to Walnut Grove Cemetery in Paris, Missouri. We have records showing he was a mail carrier in Marion county.

It is important to note that Albert's middle initial presents a mystery. In a census report, he used the middle initial of J. After some research, we found that he more often used the middle initial of G., such as on his marriage license. His father used the middle initial of G., which was verified in court documents. We still do not know what the "G." stands for. He used the given name of A. J.

The Dilts surname is of German descent. The spelling of this name has varied greatly from Diltze, Diltz, Dils, Dills, and several other variations over time. We have chosen to use the more modern version of Dilts, even though we are aware of the several earlier versions, which are also incorrect. The Germans used a different alphabet with some added letters.

We added the suffix of Jr. to his name. We found no evidence that he used the suffix of Jr., but it was added in our research and the writing of this story to keep the generations straight. Please excuse us Albert, but this helps write the story and helps our grandkids to keep history straight and remember it.

Louise B. Boren Wife of Albert G. Dilts Jr.
Born: April 1848, Missouri
Died: 24 August 1917, Monroe County, Missouri
Buried: Walnut Grove Cemetery, Paris, Missouri

Louise was the daughter of Henry Boren and Anne Elizabeth Baker of Marion County, Missouri. Henry was a wagonmaker who was born in Pennsylvania, lived for a while in Ohio, and moved to Missouri by 1846, where Louise was born. She had nine brothers and sisters.

She is buried in Walnut Grove Cemetery, Lot K276. This is a relocated, well-marked grave.

Joseph Roney Murphy
Born: 30 March 1856, Monroe County, Missouri
Died: 30 June 1930, Monroe County, Missouri
Married: 22 January 1885, Monroe County, Missouri
Buried: Pleasant Hill Cemetery, Paris, Missouri

Joseph was the son of Fielding Murphy and Elizabeth Roney of Paris, Missouri. He married Anna Maria Amanda Simon on 22 January 1885 in Monroe County. They owned and farmed on land on Middle Fork Salt River for their entire married life. They had five children:
- Thomas Edward 1885–1962
- Bessie Pauline Scott 1887–1984, who married Gorda Scott above
- Viola P. Vaughn (Paul) 1889–1985
- Ray Joy 1894–1975
- Leta Fay Vaughn (Al)
  Note: Sisters Viola and Leta married brothers Paul and Albert Vaughn.

We will later present multiple Revolutionary Patriots within the Murphy and Roney lines in this story.

As a historical note, the Murphy farm and home was located about one-fourth mile north and across the road from the Cerra Gorda Scott farm. That farm and home was owned by two Murphy generations as well as two generations of Scotts. The house no longer stands, but it is depicted in a photo later in Chapter 6.

Amanda Simon Wife of Joseph Roney Murphy
Born: 3 July 1862, Paris, Monroe County, Missouri
Died: 21 February 1954, Paris, Monroe County, Missouri
Married: 22 January 1885, Paris, Missouri
Buried: Pleasant Hill Cemetery, Paris, Missouri

Amanda was the daughter of Friedrich Eduard Wilhelm (William) Simon and Johanna Maria Eleonore Schneider of Monroe County, Missouri. William and Johanna were born and married in Berlin, Prussia, before coming to the United States in 1850 and settling in Missouri. Amanda died in 1954 in Paris while living in the Pleasant View Nursing Home. She is buried in Pleasant Hill Cemetery alongside husband Joseph Roney.

Demarquis Scott
Born: 15 August 1837, Monroe County, Missouri
Died: 11 November 1924, Paris, Missouri
Married: 1877 in Monroe County, Missouri, to Fannie Braden Crooks
Buried: Pleasant Hill Cemetery, Paris, Missouri. No stone, but next to wife Fannie Braden, who has a stone.

Demarquis was the son of Davis Scott and Nancy Ann Embree of Monroe County. He was born on the farm east of Paris and farmed in that neighborhood his entire life except for a brief expedition to Arizona to mine for gold. His name was probably carried from a brother of his mother who lived in western Monroe County.

We know little of his education, but we suspect he received at least some higher level of education, as did his brothers. The 1870 census shows him in Peeples Valley, Arizona. This town was named for A.H. Peeples, who was the leader of a group that discovered Rich Hill, a gold deposit at Weaver, Arizona, in 1863. The census reports DeMarquis as a miner with another Missouri man who said he was an engineer. The 1880 census shows DeMarquis back in Missouri. He was probably very wise to choose Arizona during the Civil War.

Demarquis married Fannie Braden Crooks in 1877 in Monroe County. They had three children:
- Anna Lenore Carter 1878–1970
- Mary Scott, b. 1879—Unknown. Died as an infant, probably a twin of Cerra Gorda.
- Cerra Gorda 1879–1963

As a remembrance of Anna Lenore, I had been married only a month or two and had a chance to meet some of the Scott family. Anna was in that group, and I will always remember that one-time meeting. She was impressive, strong, educated, and kind. She was an ordained minister with a strong command of the English language. Anna is buried in Pleasant Hill Cemetery.

DeMarquis owned a farm south of his father's farm and just north of his son's farm. The Murphy farm was close by across the road to the east. He died on 11 November 1924 and is buried in Pleasant Hill Cemetery next to Fannie's grave. Her tombstone never had his name inscribed, but he is buried next to her and is not listed as buried in that cemetery in Monroe County Historical Society records.

We have two photos of DeMarquis, one as a young man and one late in his life.

Fannie Braden Crooks Wife of DeMarquis
Born: 15 January 1855, Bath County, Kentucky
Died: 31 March 1911, Paris, Monroe County, Missouri
Buried: Pleasant Hill Cemetery, Paris, Missouri

Fannie was the daughter of Joseph Morris Crooks and Melinda Allen of Bath County, Kentucky. The Crooks lived for a short time in Illinois before moving to Audrain County, Missouri. She died at the relatively young age of fifty-six, with her cause of death being listed as pneumonia. We have an 1860 census report naming her as a daughter of Joseph and Melinda.

We note with interest Fannie's middle name of "Braden." We soon discovered it was a family name from the Crooks line and was important in the investigation of the history of the Crooks line, as you will see later in the book.

Chapter 6
Fourth Generation—Second Great-Grandparents

"If you don't know your family history, you don't know anything.
You are a leaf that doesn't know it is part of a tree."

—*Michael Crichton*

John M. "Amos" Painter Jo's second great-grandfather
Born: 25 September 1827, Martinsburg, Berkley County, Virginia
Died: 1860, Monroe County, Missouri
Married: Narcissa Stribling, 25 December 1849, Monroe City, Missouri
      Second marriage: Eleanor Greening, 14 November 1857, Monroe City
Buried: Location not proven, but probably Hawkins Cemetery

John was born in Martinsburg, Berkley County, Virginia and was the son of George Washington Painter and Sarah Ann Smith. He had seven brothers and sisters. He arrived in Florida, Missouri, around 1835 when he was eight years old. This was a large family group move to Missouri, as his parents and several of his brothers and sisters moved at the same time, settling in the Florida and Stoutsville area. His father bought a farm, and John owned land by 1850 near his father and mother.

John married Narcissa Stribling in December 1849, and they had two children: Francis Ann Dooley (Elikanah Kane) and Robert Parker. Both of these children lived long lives in the Florida and Stoutsville area. In 1853, his older brother, William, married Jane Stribling, sister of Narcissa. It is an interesting family history note that Narcissa and Jane's mother, Catherine Stribling, was the daughter of John Johnston, whose other daughter married into the Carman family, which also married into the Painter family twice. Complicated story, but we outline this relationship in our book on Patriots. Narcissa died in 1855 at the age of twenty-five. We do not know where she is buried, but possibly in the Painter plot at Florida Cemetery, in an unmarked grave.

The 1850 Monroe County census shows John Amos and his wife Narcissa living with his father and mother on the farm near Florida. By 1860, Narcissa had died and he had married Eleanor and was living on a farm near Florida, Missouri.

John Amos married Eleanor Greening on 14 November 1857. She was the daughter of Robert Greening and Elizabeth Lelva of the Stoutsville area. They had the following children:

- George H. 1829–1883, who married Alma Carman, sister of Maggie Carman, who married John T. Painter discussed above. George is buried in Hawkins Cemetery. He was fifty-four when he died, and Alma remarried and moved to another state.
- John Thomas 1860–1898
- Elizabeth M. Whelan 1861–1925. She married Benedict T. Whelan of the Stoutsville area.

The Painter connections to the Stribling and Carman families are deep and complicated. Jo and I now appreciate the relationship her father had with the gentleman Chet Carman. They were kin in so many ways that we suspect they could not explain, but I remember that relationship was strong and brotherly. I accompanied both these gentlemen to a 1993 Monroe County court session in which they requested assistance in prohibiting incursion on the Hawkins Cemetery property by a real estate developer. Their request was honored, and orders were given for the offending party to cease and desist. I had earlier assisted in documenting the many unmarked graves in that cemetery, both inside and outside the fence, and that testimony was recognized by the court.

John Amos died after September 1860 at the age of thirty-three, exact date unknown and cause of death unknown. The Monroe County 1860 census was enumerated on 25 September, in which he is represented. His probate records reflect an 1860 death and that he died intestate. His daughter Elizabeth M. was born on 21 May 1861; do the math. He owned land in both Monroe and Shelby Counties at the time of his death. This land was purchased when he was young, after his arrival in Monroe County. His probate records show several notes for loans he had made to local individuals. The Shelby County land was just north of the village of Hager's Grove and later became the site for the Hager's Grove elementary school I later attended in my second grade.

Eleanor remained on the farm but died by 1870, and we have been unable to determine the burial location of either of them after an extensive search. We have ruled out Stoutsville Cemetery as the cemetery records do not reflect their burial there, even without a headstone. They were possibly buried in Florida Cemetery, but there are no headstones for their graves there and the cemetery records do not support that contention. Hawkins Cemetery is a possible burial location, but again no headstones. They were possibly buried in one of several nearby cemeteries that were relocated during the construction of Mark Twain Lake, but if they had headstones, we would find them on the records of Walnut Grove Cemetery where those marked graves were relocated. They may be buried under Mark Twain Lake. It is interesting to note that Oliver Painter was requested by the Monroe County court to serve as a witness for the relocation of those graves, because he had relatives in them all. He probably did not realize how many relatives there really were in those cemeteries. It is our belief after discussions with Oliver about those relocations that some unmarked graves were relocated and marked as unknown. However, it is believed that several unmarked graves were not found, hence not relocated. Thus, the statement about being buried under Mark Twain Lake.

It is an interesting fact concerning the various cemetery listings that can be found. They are normally based on inventories of tombstones found and recorded by researchers. If the stone is missing or never placed, it is likely that those interred in that cemetery will not be represented in listings. Original listings such as family Bibles and old family records are helpful in finding these missing people. In the instance of Florida Cemetery, the Painter plot is adjacent to an open area with no stones standing. These stones may have been knocked down and covered or damaged and removed, or the stones were simply never placed. Florida Cemetery is a well-maintained cemetery, and the actions of people in the past are sometimes difficult to explain.

Narcissa Stribling First wife of John Amos Painter
Born: 19 August 1830 near Monroe City, Missouri
Died: 1855, Florida, Monroe County, Missouri
Married: 25 December 1849
Buried: Location not proven, but probably Florida Cemetery

Narcissa was the daughter of Tandy Stribling and Catherine Johnston of Monroe County, recently of Clark County, Kentucky. Her mother, Catherine Johnston, was the daughter of John Johnston, an early Missouri explorer, Indian fighter, and War of 1812 veteran. His father, Martin Johnston, was a Virginia Continental Line Revolutionary War soldier and survivor of the Valley Forge winter. This story is covered in depth in our *Patriots* book. The reason that Martin Johnston was presented in our *Patriots* book is not because of any kinship to Narcissa, as Jo is not descended from her, but because of her sister Mary Jacquess Johnston's marriage into the Carman family from which Emma Jo is descended. We explain that relationship later in the book.

We speculate that Narcissa might have been buried in Florida Cemetery in the Painter burial plot. There is currently no headstone for her in that plot, and there are several members of the Painter family buried there. We believe that several tombstones from that area of the cemetery were destroyed. This information was obtained during our association with the "Friends of Florida" group over many years.

Eleanor Greening Second wife of John Amos Painter
Born: June 1829, Clark County, Kentucky
Died: After 1870
Married: 14 November 1857, Monroe City, Missouri
Buried: Unknown location in Monroe county

Eleanor was the daughter of Robert Greening and Elizabeth Lelva of Clark County, Kentucky. The Greenings relocated to Monroe County, Missouri, in the early 1830s.

Eleanor was thirty-one years old at the time of John Amos's death, with two young children and pregnant with their third child. She lived until at least 1870, and no further records of her have been found. Perhaps she remarried and is accounted for by her married name in subsequent census reports and cemetery headstones.

James Henry B. Carman Jo's second great-grandfather
Born: 4 September 1828, Palmyra, Marion County, Missouri
Died: 4 February 1908
Married: 5 April 1849 in Ralls County, Missouri, to Mary Ann Schultz
Buried: Hawkins Cemetery, Monroe County

He is the son of William B. Carman and Betsy Jaquess Johnston and was born on a farm near Palmyra, Marion County, Missouri. He had eight brothers and sisters. His family moved from Harrison County, Kentucky, between 1828 and 1829 and purchased land from the Palmyra land office near that town.

James is the father of three daughters who married three Painter brothers, sons of John Amos:

- Maggie 1862–1916. Married John Thomas, Jo's great grandfather.
- Alma 186–1942. Married George H. Parker Painter.
- Mary Jane 1856–1938. Married Robert Parker Painter.

He had three other daughters who managed to not marry Painters, and three sons. He and Mary Ann had the following children:

- Marcus Linus 1850–1938. Lived in Monroe County. Grandfather of Chester discussed earlier who was a friend of Oliver Painter.
- Isaac Newton 1853–1935. Lived in Monroe County.
- Elizabeth Elner 1854–1854. Died in infancy.
- Mary Jane Painter 1856–1938. Married Robert Parker, son of John Amos Painter.
- Annie E. Leitch 1857–1937. Married John William Leitch.
- Alma Ellen Painter 1860–1942. Married George H. Painter, son of John Amos Painter.
- Margaret Lee "Maggie" Painter 1862–1916. Married John Thomas Painter, son of John Amos Painter.
- Emily Alice Scobee Dowell 1864–1936. Married James Price Scobee, then Joseph William Dowell.
- Ella E.L. "Eloees" Rouse 1866–1931. Married George T. Rouse.
- James Edward 1876–1919. Lived in Oklahoma and Missouri and is buried in Hawkins Cemetery.

He married Mary Ann Schultz Shulse in Palmyra on 5 April 1849. He later joined E company of the Fourteenth/Fifteenth Illinois Infantry during the Civil War. An obvious question is: Why serve in Illinois? First, Illinois was just across the river from Palmyra, so not that far from home. Secondly, the Marion and Monroe County area was a very strong Confederate stronghold. There would have been pressure for a young man to join one of the local Confederate militias. Illinois would have been the closest choice for a person wishing to serve the Union cause.

James was a farmer, and by 1870 he owned and farmed land near Florida, Missouri. He also owned land in Ralls County prior to moving to Monroe County. He also purchased 160 acres of Audrain County land from the Palmyra land office in 1858; however, we found no evidence of his ever living and farming that farm west of New London. It may have been a speculation purchase. He died on 8 February 1908 and is buried in a marked grave along with his wife in Hawkins Cemetery, Monroe County.

Mary Ann Schulse Wife of James Henry B. Carman
Born: 25 May 1828, Ralls County, Missouri
Died: 11 May 1882, Monroe County, Missouri
Buried: Hawkins Cemetery

Mary was the daughter of Alexander and Eleanor Shulse of New London, Ralls County, Missouri. Alexander and his wife were born in North Carolina and moved to Missouri in the mid-1820s after buying land at the Palmyra land office. Mary Ann had nine brothers and sisters.

We noted that the 160-acre farm she and James purchased in Audrain County in 1858 was relatively close to the Schulse farm near New London. Maybe they purchased for resale to one of her siblings?

Albert G. Dilts Jo's second great-grandfather
Born: 1807, Wood County, Virginia, now West Virginia
Died: Before 1880 in Ralls County, Missouri
Married: 6 December 1828 to Pamela Nancy Jacquith
        Second marriage: 7 October 1837 to Nancy Rownd
Buried: Unknown Missouri location

Albert is the father of Albert G. Dilts Jr., discussed earlier. He is the son of Henry Dilts and Christena Harmon of Indiana. He was born in Wood County, Virginia, now West Virginia, and moved with his family to Dearborn County, Indiana, around 1817. He married Pamelia Jaqueth in Dearborn on 6 December 1828. It is worthy of note that Pamelia is not the mother of Albert G. Jr. and she is from a noted colonial family. Her father, Ruben Asa Jaquith, was a War of 1812 veteran, and her grandfather, Benjamin Jaquith, was a Revolutionary War Patriot. Albert G. and Pamelia Nancy had a son, William S., before her death in 1836. She died the year William S. was born.

As with his son Albert Jr., we are uncertain of his middle initial. We have found records reflecting both G. and J.

He married Nancy Rownd on 7 October 1837 in Ripley County, Indiana. They farmed in Indiana until after 1850 and moved to New London, Ralls County, Missouri. We see he owned a small amount of land in Indiana in 1850, but later census reports show he owned no land. He apparently lived in Mississippi between 1843 and 1847 but was back in Indiana by the 1850 census and was farming there. His daughter Leah K. was born in Mississippi, as was son Albert G. Jr. in 1847.

He farmed in Marion County, but the 1864 and 1865 tax assessments show he owned hogs and was a butcher.

After the death of Albert, Nancy Rownd lived with their children in and around Hannibal, Missouri, until after 1903. Albert G. and Nancy had the following children:

- Clayton C. 1837–1923
- Helen Mcgreggor Hunt 1840–1933
- Leah 1843–?
- Albert G. Jr. 1847–1926
- Permilla 1849–Aft. 1860
- Ketchel 1851–1929
- Lewis 1853–1886
- Ann (Annie) Basketh 1855–1920
- William H. 1856–1945
- Catherine Elizabeth Griffith 1860–1935We do not know Albert's death date, but it was after the 1870 census and before the 1880 census. We are also uncertain of where he is buried.

Nancy Rownd Second wife of Albert J. Dilts above
Born: December 1816, Maryland
Died: After 1903 in Hannibal, Missouri
Married: 7 October 1837 in Ripley County, Indiana
Buried: Unknown location

Nancy was born in Maryland to Jenkins Henry Rownd and Leah Savage Evans in 1816. She was the oldest of nine children. Her family moved to the Dearborn, Indiana, area in the early 1830s, where she met and married Albert. Her father was a Maryland War of 1812 soldier and was a carpenter and later a cooper. We have been unable to prove Jenkins was her father, but census reports of Maryland and later Indiana support a female child the age of Nancy being a member of that household. She gave Maryland as her birth state on census reports, and she met Albert in Indiana while living there with her parents.

Henry Boren Father of Louise Boren, who was the wife of Albert G. Dilts Jr., so is Jo's second great-grandfather
Born: 1814 Pennsylvania
Died: After 1863, Ralls County, Missouri
Married: 25 February 1835, Washington County, Maryland, to Anne Elizabeth Baker
Buried: Unknown location

Henry gave his birth state as Pennsylvania on two census reports. He married Ann Elizabeth Baker in Maryland in 1835. We have their marriage records. Their first two children were born there. Later children were born in Ohio before their move to Ralls County, near Hannibal. We are not sure of the names of his parents, and work continues with that search. We believe his father's name was John Boren and his mother's Margaret Greenwood, but that is not proven.

Henry was working in Ralls County, Missouri, by 1850 and lived until after 1863. He and Anne Elizabeth Baker had nine children, and Louise was the next-to-youngest daughter. He listed his occupation as wagonmaker on the 1850 and 1860 census reports. We found it interesting that two sons, George and Walter, later worked in the Han wagon factory near Hannibal. One son, Henry Newton, joined the Union army early in the Civil War in Hannibal. He was wounded near Ironton, hospitalized, and later deserted. Anne Elizabeth remarried in 1864 after the death of Henry.

Henry and Anne had the following children:
- John W. 1836–? John was born in Maryland, story unknown.
- Mary Ellen Brace 1840–1901
- Henry Newton 1841–1912
- George W. 1843–1922
- Walter J. 1846–1907
- Louise B. Dilts 1848–1917
- Alexander 1850–1928
- Lucy Dixon 1852–1898
- Thomas Baker 1855–1905

Anne Elizabeth Baker Wife of Henry Boren
Born: 1817, Hagerstown, Washington County, Maryland
Died: After 1880
Married: 25 February 1835 in Washington County, Maryland
    Second marriage 1864 in Marion County, Missouri, to Daniel Pendleton
Buried: Unknown location

Ann Elizabeth is the daughter of Alexander Cooper Baker and Mary Poly Webb of Hartford County, Maryland. The Webb family is an old Maryland family with links to the Jamestown, Virginia, settlement and multiple Revolutionary War Patriots. Her father and mother moved to Marion County, Missouri, and owned a large plantation near Hannibal. They are both buried in Bellefontaine Cemetery in St. Louis, Missouri. Alexander's father, Maurice, was a Revolutionary War Patriot discussed later in this story.

We know that Anne Elizabeth was the daughter of Alexander and Mary Poly from Maryland birth records and *The History of Tuscarawas County, Ohio,* which lists their children. We know some of Alexander's children and brothers settled in Ohio, and we speculate that Henry and Elizabeth moved to Ohio at about the same time. Four of their children were born there.

Alexander and Mary Poly had moved to Marion County by 1834, and it is speculated that Henry and Anne Elizabeth followed after their children were born in Ohio. Anne remarried on 27 December 1864 after the death of Henry. She married Daniel F. Pendleton, who had been a boarder in the Boren household at the 1850 census.

Davis Scott Father of DeMarquis Scott above; Jo's second great-grandfather
Born: 7 March 1795, Lincoln County, Kentucky
Died: 18 March 1886, Monroe County, Missouri
Married: 1820 in Howard County, Missouri, to Catherine Woods
      Second marriage: 1828 in Howard County, Missouri, to Nancy Ann Embree
Buried: Scott Cemetery, Monroe County, Missouri

Davis is the father of DeMarquis Scott, discussed earlier. He was born in Lincoln County, Kentucky. His father and mother are not known. This missing family connection is what we refer to as a "brick wall." More on that later.

Davis served in the War of 1812 in Virginia in the Norfolk area for about ninety days. This was the standard militia enlistment period for that war. We do not know why he was in the Norfolk area at the age of about twenty. His unit did not fight any battles but served by being ready to block any British landings in the Norfolk port, as the British fleet had the port blockaded during part of the war. Our research seems to point out that the governor of Virginia felt the need to not be in the capital city of Richmond during the war for an obvious reason and chose to lead an expedition of militia to the Norfolk port area to dissuade the British navy from turning a port blockade into a forced landing. The governor had had enough of Norfolk in about sixty days and returned to Richmond. Those ninety-day enlistments had also expired. Davis would have likely joined the militia in Richmond.

His next known location was in Howard County, Missouri, by 1817. Even though the War of 1812 had ended by 1814, the Indians of the Missouri tribes had not received that memo. They had been stirred up by the British prior to the war, and this rivalry was slow to die down. Davis farmed, but he lived in Fort Cooper, one of two military forts in Howard County, for protection. It was 1819 before it was safe for farmers to live outside the forts. His first son, Dr. Abbot William Wood, recounted these facts for the Randolph County history project many years later. We have studied early Howard County history and can recount the violence and dangers associated with living at that location and time. We were unable to document Davis's presence then, but his son's testimony is probably accurate.

Davis bought land from the federal land office in Fayette twice in 1824 after Missouri became a state in 1821. He probably bought land he had been farming for five or six years, which was common practice then. He did not own slaves. Even though Missouri became a state in 1821, the federal land office could not sell land until a survey of the area had been completed in 1823. He probably bought that land as soon as it was available for sale. He owned two tracts of land in Howard County.

His oldest son, Dr. Abbot Wood Scott, later related to a Randolph County newspaper that his father had settled in Howard County in 1817. The Indians were extremely hostile, and he spent nights in Fort Cooper, one of two such forts in Howard County, and farmed during the day while being guarded by other settlers.

Davis married Catherine "Katy" Woods in Howard County in 1820. She had come to Missouri from Kentucky with her parents. Their only son was Abbot William Wood who was born on 22 August 1825. Katy died on 19 March 1826. Abbot later became a well-known dentist in Randolph County. Abbot's middle name is in question, as some of his records reflect Wood as his middle name; he possibly used the name out of respect for his mother's name.

Davis married Nancy Ann Embree on 25 April 1828. She had also moved with her father and mother, Thomas Burris Embree and Elizabeth Duncan, from Kentucky. Thomas soon became one of the first Monroe County settlers and lived in the Middle Grove area. More on that story later in this book.

By 1833, Davis and Nancy had purchased land and moved to Monroe County. Their farm was on the current Florida road about five miles east of Paris. Remember, Paris was formed one year before his purchase. There were few roads and no fences. Davis Scott was one of the very early settlers in Monroe County and was a farmer and cattleman. He registered his brand with the new Monroe County, as his cattle were free-range. That registration is currently on file in the Missouri History Institute in St. Louis. We found a story of one of his neighbors, John McGee Jr., who also moved from Howard County to land south of the Davis Scott farm. While this farmer was moving his family from Howard County, he and his daughter were caught on the prairie east of Paris—on what is now known as the McKamey farm—in a prairie fire and were killed. This incident occurred in January 1825, and the land he purchased was the location of the soon-to-be-established Pleasant Hill Church and Cemetery.

Davis farmed in the same location until his death in 1886. He and Nancy are buried on that farm in the Scott Cemetery. Their tombstones have been removed or destroyed, so the exact location is not certain. We know this because fifty years ago Carl and Susie Bounds recorded its location when it was intact. Those records are located in the Paris library. The Bounds spent many years documenting family cemeteries in Monroe County. We believe there were several more family graves in that cemetery than those of Davis and Nancy.

Davis and Nancy had the following nine children:
- Martha Jane Glover 1830–After 1910
- William James 1831–1903
- Thomas 1833–1882
- Elizabeth Reed 1835–1920
- Lucinda M. Baker 1836–1900
- DeMarquis 1837–1924, Jo's great-grandfather
- Mary Ann Eliza 1841–1849
- Sarah Francis Crigler 1843–1930
- Milton P. 1847–1871

We believe all the children who survived to adulthood received a good education including college. Two sons became dentists. Davis became a part owner of the Farmers Bank in Paris. He could read and write and retained a St. Louis lawyer on more than one occasion. He once filed a lawsuit against a lawyer concerning investment money. He bought and sold several farms near his home and probably helped his daughters and their husbands get a start in farming.

Upon Davis's death, his son DeMarquis, who lived near him, declared Davis had no will, so intestate probate proceedings were begun. One year later, the will was found by someone and was provided to the probate court. Davis's wife had died a few months following his death, so it was probably found in her possessions after her death. It appears he had handwritten that will, and it was signed by him and witnessed. He clearly had knowledge of the law, as he wrote his own will and it is well written.

We do not know the name of his father and mother. He gave the birthplace of his father and mother on census reports as Virginia. His obituary in the *Monroe County Mercury* reported he was born in Lincoln County, Kentucky. He also gave Kentucky as his birth state in the census reports. We continue research to find his parents.

Here is what we know about Davis Scott:
- There was a man named William Scott, about eighteen years older than Davis, who also settled in Howard County about the same time as Davis.
- This William was a farmer and slaveholder and is buried in Howard County. He was also from Lincoln County, Kentucky. We believe his father may have been named Thomas.
- Davis named his first son by Catherine Woods, Abbot William, and his first son with Nancy, William. This does not prove that the William Scott of Howard County was his father, as he was eighteen years older and single when he arrived in Howard County. They may have been brothers and he named his first two sons after his brother out of respect.In 1796 Kentucky, Lincoln County was about two-thirds of the state. It was divided over the next fifteen years into many counties.
- He probably left Lincoln County before he was a legal adult, so we do not expect to find records there in his name. We are looking for a possible father.

- We are researching all Scotts of the 1800 Lincoln County, Kentucky, particularly those with Revolutionary War records. We have narrowed the search and hope to soon solve this mystery. There are many Scotts to research. Given his writing ability, it is possible he was educated in Virginia as a lawyer. There were few schools in Kentucky in the 1800–1810 time period.
- He was clearly well educated, and that level of education was not available in Lincoln County, Kentucky, in the early 1800s. He was likely educated in Virginia. That might explain his presence in the Richmond/Norfolk area at the time of the War of 1812.

We have a photo of a man we believe to be Davis. He is well dressed in a good suit. He knew how to dress! He is wearing a pinkie ring. The date of the photo is unknown, but likely after 1850. He would have been at least fifty-five years of age, but he looked a little younger. Our photo identification software identifies him as Cerra Gorda his grandson, but it is not Cerra. It is definitely a Scott gentleman with a dark complexion. Others have identified the gentleman as his oldest son, Dr. Abbot, but we have a photo of him also, and they are not the same men.

Richard Scott, grandson of Cerra Gorda, did extensive research to identify the parents of Davis. We are in possession of that work, and we will eventually solve this mystery. We believe his father served in the Revolutionary War and received a land grant in Kentucky. We simply need to research all Scott soldiers receiving a land grant in Kentucky.

We believe that the stories of this family add to our knowledge and understanding of the Scotts. Here are some facts we have uncovered about their children and grandchildren listed above:

Davis's and Nancy's oldest daughter, Martha Jane Glover, married a man named Glover, but we have been unable to further identify this man. They had three children before his death or disappearance:

- Mary 1854–1864
- Joseph H. 1855–?
- John Alfred 1858–1864

Both Mary and John Alfred died in August 1864 and are buried with marked graves at Pleasant Hill Cemetery. Perhaps they died from the diphtheria epidemic? Joseph can be found in the Davis Scott household until after 1860, but no later records can be found. Perhaps he died also and is buried in Scott Cemetery?

Martha Jane and her children lived with Davis and Nancy until the children's deaths and the death of Davis and Nancy. Martha Jane then lived with brother DeMarcus until her death around 1910. We cannot find her buried in Pleasant Hill Cemetery, so we suspect she may have been buried in Scott Cemetery, but that is a guess.

Son William James (1831–1903) married Mary J. Bell of Monroe County in 1856, and they had nine children. Mary died in 1875, and William married Elizabeth in 1897. William and Mary farmed in the Middle Grove area and later near Keytsville, Chariton County.

After the death of Mary, he owned and farmed land in Randolph County, near Clifton Hill. His older brother Abbot would have been a neighbor.

Son Thomas (1833–1882) became a dentist by 1860 and practiced in Paris and later in Fulton, Missouri. We are not sure he ever practiced in Fulton, but he was probably committed to the state hospital there. He never married and his burial location is unknown. We found a newspaper article indicating he was a patient there.

Their daughter Elizabeth "Eliza" Preston (1835–1920) married Preston Reed in 1853, and they had six children. They farmed in Linn County, and she later lived in St. Joseph, Missouri, after the death of Preston.

Daughter Lucinda M. Baker (1836–1900) married Isaac Baker in 1883 when she was forty-seven years old. She had lived with her father and mother until that time. They had no children.

Son DeMarquis (1837–1924) was discussed above.

Daughter Mary Ann "Eliza" (1841–1849) died at eight years of age and may be buried in the Scott family cemetery.

Daughter Sarah Francis Crigler (1843–1930) married John W. Crigler, and they farmed in southern Audrain County and had four children. She is buried in the Mexico, Missouri, Elmwood Cemetery.

Son Sergeant Major Milton P. (1847–1871). We have found few records of the life of the youngest son of Davis and Nancy Scott. Our first hint of his life other than the 1850 and 1860 census reports, occurred when we discovered that "Find-A-Grave" records his burial in Old Martinsburg Confederate Cemetery of Martinsburg, Missouri. This site alleges that he died in 1871 and is buried at that cemetery, and that he served in the Twenty-third Missouri Confederate Regiment as a sergeant major. Being somewhat familiar with Missouri Civil War units, we realized there was no such unit. There was certainly a Missouri Civil War Union Volunteer Regiment with this designation, but not a Confederate regiment.

This particular Missouri regiment was formed in Linn County, Missouri, in early 1862. It fought a hard and brutal war. It was quickly assigned to the Tennessee department and fought in the Battle of Shiloh in Tennessee. Most of the regiment was either killed or captured during that battle, and even the regimental commander was killed. The prisoners were transported eventually to Georgia and then returned to St. Louis, Missouri, for exchange later in 1862. The unit was quickly reorganized and again assigned to operations in Missouri and on to Tennessee and assigned to the campaign with General Sherman in his march to Atlanta and on to the east coast. This unit saw a lot of combat and was disbanded at the end of the war.

Our search of rosters of the unit yielded one roster showing a Milton Scott enlisting in Linn, Missouri, in "F" company—commanded by Captain Rice Morris—as a private, later becoming a sergeant major. If this is the correct Milton Scott, he would have enlisted in April 1863 in Macon, Missouri, at the age of maybe fifteen or sixteen. Find-A-Grave reflects his rank and that he died of injuries from the war.

While there are records pertaining to this unit, most are far from complete. We cannot explain his burial in a cemetery in southern Audrain County.

Nancy Ann Embree Second wife of Davis Scott
Born: About 1811, Clark County, Kentucky
Died: 13 May 1886, Monroe County, Missouri
Married: 24 April 1828, Howard County, Missouri
Buried: Scott farm in Monroe County in unknown location

Nancy is the daughter of Thomas Burris Embree and Elizabeth "Betsy" Duncan of Clark County, Kentucky. Thomas was born in 1774 in Orange County, Virginia, and Elizabeth was born in Orange County in 1776. Thomas and Elizabeth were married in Clark County in 1797 after moving with their families from Virginia. Thomas served in the military for the War of 1812 in Kentucky. They moved to Randolph/Monroe County prior to 1830. Thomas and Elizabeth were among the first two settlers along with Ezra Fox in Monroe County. I remember being taught this in school.

Nancy and Davis were married in 1828 in Howard County. An interesting note is that one of her many brothers was named Demarcus; he died in 1845. Was her son DeMarcus, born in 1837, named after her brother?

Joseph Morris Crooks Father of Fannie Braden Crooks; Jo's second great-grandfather
Born: 1813–14 Bath County, Kentucky
Died: After 1866, Audrain County, Missouri
Married: 7 June 1837 in Morgan County, Illinois, to Melinda Allen
Buried: Unknown location, probably in Audrain County, Missouri

We are uncertain who Joseph's mother and father are. We have extensive research done by Richard Scott in 1979 and 1980 involving both professional researchers and informal family groups, as well as our own recent research. Here are proven facts concerning Joseph:
- We see him in the 1840 and 1850 census records for Bath County, Kentucky.
- We have his marriage records for his marriage to Melinda Allen in 1834.
- We have property records for property he and Melinda purchased in Bath County in 1848 and 1849.
- We have birth records for the birth of daughter Fannie Braden in Bath County.
- He and Melinda are both, along with their children, living in Salt River Township in Audrain County, Missouri, by 1856.
- The last-known records of Joseph are the Audrain excise tax records in 1866.

Although we are uncertain of his father, we are relatively certain of the names of both his grandfather and great-grandfather. We have Bible records of James Crook III of Virginia listing his sons as well as father James Crook Jr. of New Jersey and Pennsylvania.

We have researched all sons of both James Jr. and James III and their grandsons, and have been unable to positively link Joseph to that line, but as Joseph can be linked to Bath County, Kentucky, the line of James Crook III can be placed in that and surrounding Kentucky Counties in many ways. We have a candidate, and we have eliminated all other possible fathers from this family line from the results of our research and study.

James Crooks III (1745–1823) had three sons by his first wife, Anne Braden. He and his sons settled in Kentucky after the death of Anne Braden. These sons were:
- Uzal 1774–1824. Settled in Bath County.
- Robert Braden 1780–1845. Settled in Bath County.
- James IV 1786-1813, Settled in Bath County after 1800. His mother, Anne Braden, died within thirty days of his birth.

James III remarried Elizabeth Warford after the death of Anne. Their sons were:
- Abraham 1788–1859. Settled in Greenup County, Kentucky.
- Henry 1791–1818. Settled in Illinois and had no children.
- Job 1792–1819. Never married.
- William 1800–1875. Not married until after the birth of Joseph.
- John Turley 1807–1896. Too young to be Joseph's father.

We eliminated both Uzal and Robert Braden as the father of Joseph due to the birth of their children. Robert had no sons, and Uzal's children are well documented and born in years that eliminate Joseph as a sibling.

We initially eliminated James IV as the father of Joseph because he was killed in May 1813 in the War of 1812. James IV married Abigal Frier in 1809 in Clark County, Kentucky. This death date of May 1813 seems to bring his being the father of Joseph into question, but the birth year of Joseph is based mostly on ages given in various census reports. He might well have been born in 1813 instead of 1814.

James IV's wife, Abigal Frier, remarried in 1816 to Thomas Wagle of Clark County. He was a postmaster of that area. We see the 1830 census containing a male youth under fifteen that might well be Joseph, but that is speculation. What we do know is that Thomas Wagle married Mary Cox in November 1837, possibly after the death of Abigal Frier. The spelling of her given name is based on her marriage records and a census report.

Joseph probably never knew his father, and his mother was likely dead before he was twenty-two. We know that his uncle Robert Braden was in Bath County for the 1830 and 1840 census and had no sons. He was a close neighbor of Joseph in 1840. He was probably a man with substantial resources, and we can speculate he had a role in the raising of Joseph Morris. Robert had many slaves and large land holdings. After all, Joseph named his daughter Fannie Braden either after Robert Braden or his grandmother Anne Braden, or both. Joseph's grandfather James III was living in Bath County in 1820, and we see a young male living with him, the correct age group for Joseph Morris.

Joseph married Melinda Allen in 1837in Morgan County, Illinois. We have a copy of that marriage record. They lived in Bath County and were landowners. We have copies of those land transactions. Land in Bath County was then and is now very expensive land. Maybe uncle Robert helped them in some way. He and Melinda had moved to Salt River Township in Audrain County, Missouri, by 1856. Their son Newton Monroe was born there in 1856. He and Melinda had nine children, seven surviving to adulthood:

- Lucy Jane Cheathan 1837–1902. Died in Oklahoma William 1843–?
- Henrietta Doty 1845–? Settled in Audrain Missouri
- Joseph Morris Jr. 1848–1935. A minister who settled in Colorado
- James H. 1850–After 1900. Died in Colorado
- Benjamin 1853–?
- Fannie Braden 1855–1911. Married DeMarcus Scott
- Newton Monroe 1856–1916 Died in Kentucky
- M.E. 1860–?

We have not been able to find Joseph's burial location; however, we assume it is in Monroe or Audrain County. He and his family lived and farmed in Salt River Township of northern Audrain County.

The story of Joseph Morris Crooks has been developed over fifty years and is the result of a couple of professional researchers and several other Crooks family members who assisted Richard Scott. We merely followed the advice of two professionals who recommended that Richard Scott develop the genealogy of the James Crooks families. More proof is needed to positively link Joseph Morris to James Crooks IV, but I think Richard Scott would be encouraged if he could see this work. Thanks Richard!

As a matter of interest, there are multiple Revolutionary War Patriots in the James Crooks lines. We have not included these men in our *Patriots* book due to insufficient proof of the Joseph Morris and James IV relationship. Work continues. We will present what we know of James Crooks III and James Jr. in subsequent generation chapters below.

Melinda Allen Wife of Joseph M. Crooks; Jo's second great-grandmother
Born: 1818, Bath County, Kentucky
Died: After 1880, Monroe County, Missouri
Married: 7 June 1837 in Morgan, Illinois
Buried: Unknown location. Speculation is Scott Cemetery in Monroe County.

Melinda is the daughter of George Allen and Barbara "Barbary" Myers of Bath, Kentucky. She is the fourth of four children. Her mother, Barbary, is the daughter of Henrich Henry Myers, also a Patriot featured in the *Patriots* book. More on this story later.

We are not certain of Melinda's death date or burial location; however, we find her as a neighbor to Davis and DeMarcus Scott in Monroe County for the 1880 census. She was living with her son William and his wife. Her daughter Fannie Braden was the wife of DeMarcus Scott; they were also neighbors. We will speculate that she may be buried in the Scott family cemetery, which was destroyed in the late twentieth century. Her name was not recorded in the Carl Bounds inventory of that cemetery, but maybe there was never a grave marker erected over her grave. Another possible location would be the cemetery of her husband.

Fielding Murphy Father of Joseph Roney Murphy; Jo's second great-grandfather
Born: 20 March 1824, Oldham County, Kentucky
Died: 4 November 1900, Monroe County, Missouri
Married: 8 September 1857 in Oldham County, Kentucky, to Elizabeth Roney
  Second marriage: Mary Catherine Foree Roney, married 3 May 1892
Buried: Pleasant Hill Cemetery, Monroe County, Missouri

Fielding was the son of John Lewis Murphy Jr. and Betsy Ashby of Oldham County, Kentucky. His grandfather was John Murphy, a Revolutionary War Patriot presented in our *Patriots* book. His mother, Betsy, was the daughter of Fielding Ashby, also a Revolutionary War Patriot. The Ashby family produced more than twenty Patriots in that war and are featured in the *Patriots* book. This is a storied family with multiple connections to George Washington.

Fielding married Elizabeth Roney in Oldham County, Kentucky, on 11 September 1851. Elizabeth was the daughter of Ellis Roney and Maria Oglesby, also of Oldham County. The father of Ellis was Hercules Roney II, who was a Revolutionary War Patriot. There are several other Patriots from this line that we will discuss later.

Two years after their marriage, Fielding and Elizabeth moved to Monroe County, Missouri. They farmed east of Paris where their children were born and raised. Fielding died in 1900, and he and Elizabeth are buried in Pleasant Hill Cemetery east of Paris, Missouri.

Their first farm was located near the DeMarquis Scott farm, and their second farm was located across the farm road to the east. This farm later became the property of Cerra Gorda Scott and later Jr. Scott.

Fielding and Elizabeth had the following children:
- John Ellis 1852–1942
- Mary S. 1854–1855
- Joseph Roney 1856–1930
- James W. 1858–1870
- William Fielding 1859–1912
- William 1861–?
- Thomas 1863–1920

Fielding married Mary Catherine Foree/Roney in 1892 after the death of Elizabeth. They had no children from this marriage.

Sitting: Fielding Murphy, Mary Catherine Foree Roney Murphy.
Standing: Possibly Arthur Roney, (son of Mary), Ella Porter (wife of John Roney), John Roney (son of Mary), remainder are unknowns.

This photo is of Fielding and wife Mary Catherine and several other family members and was probably taken after their marriage in 1892. The photo was taken in front of their house, later owned by son Joseph Roney and later by Cerra and then Jr. Scott.

Elizabeth Roney Wife of Fielding Murphy; Jo's second great-grandmother
Born: 4 December 1823, Oldham County, Kentucky
Died: 6 February 1882, Monroe County, Missouri
Married: 8 September 1857 in Oldham County, Kentucky, to Fielding Murphy
Buried: Pleasant Hill Cemetery, Paris, Missouri

Elizabeth was the daughter of Ellis Roney and Maria Oglesby of Oldham County, Kentucky. The lineage of her father was mentioned above, and her mother is a descendant of a Revolutionary War father, Jesse Oglesby, who will also be discussed later. Her mother, Celia Witt, also descended from a Patriot—David Witt, later discussed.

We should note that after 1900, some Roney family members chose to spell the name "Rooney." There is no historical precedent for this spelling; it is just a preference.

The Fielding Murphy Family Circa: 1892–1900

Mary Catherine Foree/Roney Second wife of Fielding Murphy
Born: 7 December 1842 in Kentucky
Died: 25 December 1922 in Jackson County, Missouri
Married: 1861 in Monroe County, Missouri, to Joseph Franklin Roney
   Second marriage: 3 May 1892 to Fielding Murphy
Buried: Jackson County, Missouri.

She lived with a son after the death of Fielding. She had four children by the first marriage.

We were unaware of this marriage between Fielding and Mary until we found the above photo. We speculated that it was Fielding and his family and were certain of the location, given that we had family photos of later generations at the same location. That location has been confirmed by other family members. Realizing that Elizabeth had died in 1882, and knowing that family photos taken with a "box camera" in 1882 would not have been probable, we undertook the solution to that mystery. That's when we discovered his later marriage.

The photo contains other people, likely family members. One man is wearing a black-and-white-striped outer garment. I would call it a jail uniform and am not sure what else to call it. We will continue our search to identify those people. There is probably "the rest of the story" to be told.

Mary Catherine was the daughter of Joseph Foree and Caroline A. Shrader. She married Joseph Franklin Roney in 1861, and he died in 1879. He was from Oldham County, Kentucky, and was certainly related to Elizabeth Roney, Fielding's first wife (maybe a brother).

Friedrich Eduard Wilhelm "William" Simon Father of Anna Maria Amanda Simon Murphy; Jo's second great-grandfather
Born: 25 April 1820, Brandenburg, Westfalen, Prussia
Died: 1 October 1910, Paris, Monroe County, Missouri
Married: 1849 in Germany to Johanna Maria Eleonore Schneider
Buried: Pleasant Hill Cemetery, Paris, Missouri

The name gives away the national heritage of "William." He was born in Katholisch, Brandenburg, Westfalen, Prussia, to Johann Heinrich Simon and Sophia Ehbrecht. He married Johanna Maria Eleonore Schneider 1849 in Prussia, and they arrived in the United States on 23 October 1850. They arrived on the *Ocean Queen* from Bremen, Germany, to New Orleans. They received their citizenship in 1855 in Monroe County, Missouri. They farmed in Monroe County until their deaths. William died on 1 October 1910, and he is buried in Pleasant Hill Cemetery east of Paris. We believe that William might have had a previous marriage from which a son was born. His name was Friedrich Wilhelm Hermann, and he was born in 1846 and died in 1863 in Prussia.

We have a news article of 6 May 1892 from the *Moberly Monitor-Index* in which he and his family celebrated his seventy-second birthday. There were forty-eight friends and family in attendance. While this large group was being seated for the meal, William and son-in-law Joe Murphy slipped into the kitchen and hid the turkey. This article stated he and his family resided near Palmyra for a few years before moving to Monroe County. The 1860 Monroe County census shows his farm ownership in Monroe County.

William and Maria had the following nine children:
- Augustus Henry 1851–1932
- Wilhelm Eduard Aswalt 1853–1941
- Anna 1855–?
- Friedrich Wilhelm Rudolf 1859–1919
- Paul Albert Wilhelm 1860–1932
- Anna Maria Amanda 1862–1954
- Eduard Oswald 1865–1940
- Charles L. 1868–?
- Eduard Wilhelm Bruno 1868–1955

Johanna Maria Eleonore Schneider Wife of Friedrich Eduard Wilhelm Simon
Born: 23 September 1822 in Prussia
Died: 4 May 1901, Paris, Monroe County, Missouri
Married: 1849 in Prussia to Friedrich Eduard Wilhelm "William" Simon
Buried: Pleasant Hill Cemetery, Paris, Missouri

"Joanna" was born in Brandenburg, Prussia, to Gorrgried Schneider and Dorthea Grubeln. She used both the given names of Joanna and Eleonore at different times, but Joanna seemed to be the most common.

She arrived in New Orleans with Friedrich and their oldest son Augustus Henry in October 1850. Most of their nine children remained in the Monroe County area and raised large families. We believe that most Monroe County Simons can trace their lineage to William and Joanna. Their daughter Ana Maria Amanda is Jo's great-grandmother.

Virgil E. and Emma Jo Painter Raines

Chapter 7
Fifth Generation—Third Great-Grandparents

"Genealogy is about proving that bad family traits came from the other side of the tree."

—Unknown researcher

More in-depth information has been given to this family lineage despite the fact that most of them are not direct ancestors to Emma Jo. They are, however, cousins and second cousins, many in Missouri, that we have contact with and may possibly have an interest in these shared relationships.

George Washington Painter Father of John M. "Amos" Painter; Jo's third great-grandfather
Born: 15 July 1784 in Martinsburg, Berkley County, Virginia
Died: 15 September 1853 in Florida, Monroe County, Missouri
Married: 10 April 1809 in Berkley County, Virginia, to Sarah Ann Smith
Buried: Florida Cemetery, Florida, Missouri

George was the son of Jacob Painter Sr. and Eve Catherine Seibert of Martinsburg, Berkley County, Virginia. Berkley County was a Virginia County until West Virginia gained statehood in 1863, so it is accurate to attribute his birth state as Virginia. His father was a first-generation American from Pennsylvania who settled in Virginia soon after serving in the Revolutionary War.

George gave his birth state as Virginia in the 1850 census, so we assume that to be correct. However, he was born the year his family arrived in Virginia from Pennsylvania, as we find his father, Jacob, on a 1783 Pennsylvania tax list. His father wasted no time leaving Pennsylvania after discharge from the army, also in 1783. A land grant probably affected that decision. Did the colony of Pennsylvania give Revolutionary War land grants in Virginia? The answer is both yes and no. Part of what is now West Virginia was a contested area that both Pennsylvania and Virginia claimed prior to the war. That issue was settled during the first Congress, but the grants had been issued. Virginia was still giving land grants in Kentucky well after it became a state, and they got away with that. Daniel Boone learned that the hard way. We are unable to confirm the middle name of Washington. Official documents such as marriage records and probate records do not support this contention. He named his son George Washington Jr., who used the Jr. suffix in the 1850 census while living with his father. We see that several grandsons were also given the name of George Washington.

George married Sarah Ann Smith in Berkley County on 10 April 1809, and they had the following nine children, all born in Virginia:

- Jacob 1810–1895
- Nancy Denny 1812–1853
- Mary Ann Cole 1812–1848
- Elizabeth Thomas 1817–1853
- Sarah Ann Harvin 1820–1860
- George Washington Jr. 1823–1852
- William Samuel 1825–1876
- John M. "Amos" 1827–1860
- Samuel H. 1829–1893

George served in the Virginia Artillery Militia for ninety days during the War of 1812. The ninety-day enlistment period was typical for militia enlistments during that war, and we could find no battles attributed to that unit. During our research of his father, we found that he may have made a rifle for George, who used it during the war. We found some evidence that his father had worked at an armory in Pennsylvania prior to the Revolutionary War, but that is not a documented story.

We could not determine the exact date of George and his family's relocation from Virginia to Monroe County, but the 1840 Missouri census has him in Monroe County. He certainly arrived between 1829 and 1840, as his last child, Samuel, was born in 1829 in Virginia.

What appears to be a normal migration from Virginia was probably far from that. Not to say that many settlers did not make that migration, it's just most of those migrations involved a one-generation stopover in Kentucky or Ohio. George wasted no time—they just moved one thousand miles from what is now West Virginia to Monroe County, Missouri, in the 1830s over what had been unfriendly Indian country just a few years earlier.

We have pondered that move for some time, recounting our first trip to Virginia by car in 1965. At that time the Interstate system was in early construction and certainly did not exist in the West Virginia mountains and western Pennsylvania. We quickly learned that western Pennsylvania and the Wheeling, West Virginia, area were known for ten months of winter and two months of poor skiing. Weather was always a factor in that area, even 130 years after the George Painter journey. It was a long way to Missouri.

We first considered that their trip involved river travel. They could have taken a boat down the Monongahela River to the Ohio River and on to the Mississippi and up that river to St. Louis. That route had been used since the 1770s. The most likely route seems to be the first national U.S. road. The National Road was built between 1811 and 1837. Early parts of this road were known as the Cumberland Pike. The intent of the U.S. government was for the road to terminate in St. Louis, but it stopped in Vandalia, Illinois, in 1837, then the capitol of Illinois. It was about one hundred miles farther to St. Louis. This road consisted of sections of many older trails—some Indian trails and some surveyed by explorers such as Christopher Gist, a Raines family ancestor. Completed or not, the road existed in the 1830s, and it presented the Painter family a relatively safe route to Missouri, and we believe this was their route to Missouri. Road maps did not exist, and major rivers did not have bridges. The Ohio River bridge at Wheeling, West Virginia, was not built until 1849.

George and Sarah's oldest son, Jacob, purchased land in Shelby County, Missouri, in November 1837 and again in April 1838. Jacob was single and about twenty-seven years old in 1837. As the oldest son, his father might have sent him ahead to locate farmland in Missouri, but that is speculation, as the first purchase was in partnership with a man named Hawkins, of a well-known Monroe County family. Perhaps the family had completed the trip to Missouri by 1837 and Jacob was merely getting started with two hundred acres of Shelby County land just north of North Fork Salt River and the village of Hager's Grove. Jacob married in 1840 and bought a farm in Monroe County near Stoutsville and lived there for the remainder of his life. We found it interesting that his father, George, also bought a farm in Shelby County, a few miles north of Jacob's farm. We have no evidence that George ever lived on or farmed that land. It was part of his final estate.

What we are certain of is that George bought a farm near Florida and farmed there the remainder of his life. He would have been over forty-five years old at the time of his move with his entire family, so it is easy to imagine that the move was to establish his family where land was more available.

George died on 25 September 1853 at the age of sixty-nine on his farm near Florida, and he is buried in Florida Cemetery in a marked grave. Jo and I visit his grave site every year and have participated in historical re-enactments there.

His Monroe County probate files show that his wife, Sarah, was the co-executor and that he was in debt to an amount exceeding the value of his estate less real estate. His debts eventually resulted in the forced sale of his land. The first sale, by order of the Monroe County court, was 180 acres of land in Shelby County, Missouri. It was the N.E. qtr. of Section 10 Township 58, Range 12 W. consisting of about 180 acres. This land was about eight miles east of Bethel. The second sale was Monroe County property consisting of about 114 acres. That was the W. half of the S.E. qtr. of Section 17, Township 55, Range 8. The second part of this land was Section 20, Township 55, Range 8. This farm contained the house and outbuildings and is located just east of current State Highway 107 about four miles north of Florida and three miles east of Stoutsville. We believe that sons William, Jacob, and Samuel bought the land when it was sold. His wife, Sarah, bought the house. The land sales netted $2,670.00, which more than paid the outstanding debt of $753.00.

We could not help but notice that debts owed by George were to sons William, Jacob, and Samuel. It is true he owed a few dollars to local stores, but the bulk of the debt was to sons. It seems unusual for a father to borrow money from sons, especially when they probably had little cash to loan. Perhaps this was a method of passing his land to desired family members without writing a will, which would be public knowledge. That is speculation.

George and Sarah's eight children, except George W. Jr., remained in Monroe County and had large families. This summarizes the history of these family groups:

Jacob 1810–1895. He married Hannah Ann Thomas (1811–1908), and they had eight children. They farmed near Stoutsville and lived long lives and are buried in Stoutsville Cemetery. Their children were:
- Naomi Virginia Starret/Clapper 1844–1931
- Mary F. Brusker 1846–1934
- Amos 1847–?
- Malvina Jane 1850–?
- Sarah Jane Ogle 1853–1920
- George Oliver 1854–1920
- Albert Demoss 1858–1934
- Luella Hall 1861–1928

Mary Ann Cole 1812–1848. She married Joseph Cole, and they had four children. She and Joseph married in Berkley, Virginia, and moved to Missouri with her parents and siblings. She died at the age of thirty-six and may be buried in Florida Cemetery, but no headstone has been found. Their children were:
- George Washington 1834–1895
- Malvina 1836–1878George N. 1837–?
- Mary A. 1846–?

Nancy Denny 1815–1853. She married George William Denny (1811–1852) in 1839 in Monroe County. She died the same year as her father, and it is possible she is buried in Florida Cemetery, but again, no headstone has been found. Her husband died the previous year and may also be buried in Florida Cemetery.

Elizabeth Thomas 1817–1853. She married John Thomas (1817–1887) in Monroe County in 1840. They had eight children, several dying in infancy. She died at the age of thirty-six after the birth of their last child. She is buried in Florida Cemetery with a headstone, as are five of their children. John later moved to Illinois and remarried. We speculate that John Thomas Painter, son of Elizabeth's brother John Amos, was named after this John Thomas. John and Elizabeth's children were:
- Eliza Ellen 1836–1917
- George Washington 1841–1841. Buried in Florida Cemetery.
- Perry 1842–1842. Buried in Florida Cemetery.
- Sarah R. 1844–1895. Buried in Florida Cemetery.
- Samuel R. 1846-1895
- Cynthia Ann 1848–1850. Buried in Florida Cemetery.
- John Wesley 1850–1937
- Stillborn 1853-?

Sarah Ann Harvin 1820–1860. Sarah married George Washington Harvin on 4 October 1846 in Monroe County, Missouri. George was a farmer, and they were next door neighbor to John M. "Amos" Painter, brother of Sarah. Early in the Civil War, George joined a Confederate guerilla unit commanded by Colonel Porter, a very colorful leader. This unit operated mainly in Monroe and Marion Counties and generated the interest of Union commanders. In July 1862 a Union regiment cornered several soldiers of the Porter regiment near Florida. At least two prisoners were taken, and George was one of those two, as was his brother-in-law Samuel H. Painter. Samuel was the brother of Sarah and John M. "Amos" Painter. These two prisoners were taken to the Gratiot and Myrtle Street Prison in St. Louis. George died there of disease on 2 December that year. His brother-in-law Samuel was transferred to the Alton, Illinois, prison and spent the remainder of the war there.

George and Sarah Ann had six children:
- Laura E. 1847–?
- John W. 1848–1934
- Thomas E. 1852–?
- George Washington 1854–?
- Cynthia Ann Painter 1855–1930. Married George Oliver Painter, son of Jacob Painter, listed above.
- Susannah 1857– ?

George Jr. 1823–1852. He may have left Missouri after the 1850 census for the California Gold Rush. Family lore has it he disappeared there. Death date is likely 1851 or 1852. He never married.

William Samuel 1825–1876. He married Jane Stribling, sister of Narcissa, who married John M. "Amos" Painter in 1853. Brothers William S. and John Amos married sisters.

William and Jane farmed in South Fork Township of Monroe County, near Santa Fe. He is buried in Santa Fe's South Fork Cemetery. He and Jane had eight children, five of which survived to adulthood. Oliver Painter's notes show that Cordelie, Sarah Ann, and Clara W. were buried in Scobee Cemetery, which was relocated to Paris by the Corps of Engineers. Mark Twain Lake now covers that old cemetery site. Those were probably unmarked graves, so we do not believe they were relocated. Their children were:
- Mary Elizabeth Smith 1854–1906
- William Mace 1857–1933
- Nancy Catherine "Kate" Hale 1859–1929
- Cordelie Hildred 1860–1863
- Henry 1864–1956
- Sarah Ann 1867–1870
- Clara W. 1867–1870
- Stella J. Coppedge 1869–1889

John M. "Amos" 1827–1860. Discussed above in fourth generation as Jo's second great-grandfather.

Samuel H. 1829–1893. Samuel was the last of the George W. Painter children and was born in Virginia. He married America Ann Nesbit in 1853 in Monroe County, Missouri. He farmed in the Stoutsville area for his entire life. He joined the 1st Northeast Missouri Confederate regiment on 2 July 1862 and was soon captured and imprisoned in St. Louis, Missouri. He was soon moved to the Alton, Illinois, prison, where he spent the remainder of the war. He and America Ann had ten children, six of which survived until adulthood. They are:

- George Washington 1853–1854
- Amanda Virginia Kennett 1855–1940
- Thomas Jefferson 1857–1858
- Emily 1859–1870
- Eamilius Oscar 1859–1936
- Samuel F. 1861–1861
- Nancie Elizabeth "Nina" Jones 1862–1930
- James William "Will" 1865–1923
- John Chauncey 1869–1928
- Amelia Watson 1873–1899

Both Samuel and America Ann, along with several of their children, are buried in Stoutsville Cemetery.

Sarah Ann Smith Wife of George Washington Painter; Jo's third great-grandmother
Born: 5 October 1785, Berkley, James County, Virginia
Died: 10 November 1857, Florida, Monroe County, Missouri
Married: 10 April 1809 in Berkley, James County, Virginia, to George Painter
Buried: Florida Cemetery, Florida, Missouri

Sarah is the daughter of John Smith and Elizabeth Giles of Berkley, James County, Virginia. Her father was born in Essex County, Massachusetts, and her mother in Maryland.

She and George were married in 1809 in Virginia, and she is buried in Florida Cemetery in Florida, Missouri.

Robert Greening Jr. Father of Eleanor Greening, second wife of John M. "Amos" Painter
Born: 1794, Albemarle County, Virginia
Died: After 1860, Stoutsville, Monroe County, Missouri
Married: 7 May 1817 in Fayette, Kentucky, to Elizabeth Lelva
Buried: Location unknown, but possibly Stoutsville Cemetery

Robert Greening Jr. was born in Albemarle County, Virginia, to Robert Greening and Sarah Dowell of Albemarle. By 1800, he was living with his parents in Clark County, Kentucky. He married Elizabeth Lelva on 7 May 1817 in Fayette, Kentucky. They farmed in Clark County until 1840, when they moved to Monroe County, Missouri, after buying a small farm at the Palmyra Federal Land Office. He died in Monroe County after the 1860 census. Robert and Elizabeth had the following children:

- Thomas D. 1820–1903
- Eleanor Painter 1829–1870. Wife of John M. "Amos" Painter
- William 1831–1917
- Editha Yates 1834–1910
- Henry Clay 1837–1880

Eleanor is listed by name on her father's 1850 census.

We are unsure of the burial location of either Robert or Elizabeth, but Stoutsville Cemetery is a likely location.

William B. Carman Father of James Henry B. Carman; third great-grandfather of Jo
Born: 1791, York, Westchester County, New York
Died: 17 April 1874, Warren, Marion County, Missouri
Married: 27 August 1814 in Harrison, Kentucky, to Betsy Jaquess Johnston
     Second marriage: Sarah Calvin, 18 April 1844, Ralls County, Missouri
Buried: Carman Cemetery, Marion County, Missouri

William is the son of Henry Carman and Elizabeth C. Kom of Westchester County, New York. He had two brothers. His father, Henry, was a Revolutionary War Patriot. We tell his story in the *Patriots* book, and we will also discuss him later in this story.

We cannot prove the relationship of William as the son of Henry. It is that simple and is that complicated. Henry died relatively young and intestate. We are collaborating with a descendant of William who is a New York publisher and experienced researcher to prove this relationship. We will include Henry later in this project based on the certainty of what we believe we will find. It is not a wild guess.

William B. found himself in Kentucky by 1812 by the age of twenty-one as a soldier in the Kentucky second regiment of volunteers under the command of Colonel Jennings. That was a state regiment as opposed to local militia, and it offered 360-acre land grants for service as well as several hundred dollars as a signing bonus. That grant would have been a great start for a poor young man. Maybe those rewards drew him from New York to Kentucky.

He was living in Harrison County, Kentucky, by 1814 at the end of the War of 1812 when he married Betsy Jaquess Johnston. They had moved to near Palmyra, Marion County, Missouri by 1830 and farmed there for the remainder of his life. His wife Betsy died on 16 February 1841, and he married Sarah Calvin on 18 April 1844 in Ralls County, Missouri. William and Betsy had the following children:

- Paulina J. Pierce 1817–1903
- Elizabeth A. Dearing 1817–before 1852
- Nancy W. Gibbons 1822–1906
- Harriet Heckart 1825–1900
- Mary Jane Nelson 1825–1899
- Emily Ann Maston 1827–1869
- William B. 1828–1874
- James Henry B. 1830–1900

William and second wife, Sarah Calvin, had no children. She died in 1877 and is buried in Carman Cemetery in Marion County.

Betsy Jaquess Johnston First wife of William B. Carman; Jo's third great-grandmother
Born: 1791, New York
Died: 16 February 1841, Marion County, Missouri
Married: 27 August 1814 in Kentucky to William B. Carman
Buried: Carman Cemetery, Marion County, Missouri

Betsy was the daughter of John Johnston and Francis Hawkins of New York. She was living in Kentucky by the time she was sixteen. She first married Isaac Jaquess in 1812, who was soon killed in the War of 1812. She then married William Carman on 27 August 1814 in Harrison County, Kentucky, and continued to use the Jaquess name with the Carman name.

We are simply uncertain of Betsy's birth location. Her father and mother lived in Culpepper County, Virginia, in their later lives. Other researchers claim the New York as the birth state. We have researched the Johnston family and found New York connections, but no proof. What we are certain of is that her father is John Johnston. He signed her marriage bond for her marriage to William B. Carman in 1814 in Harrison County, Kentucky. Maybe Betsy knew William B. from the New York connection?

Her father, John Johnston, was a War of 1812 veteran and was an early explorer in the Missouri territory, receiving a Spanish land grant. He worked with several Indian tribes in Missouri. His father, Martin Johnston, was a Revolutionary War Patriot who is discussed later in this story.

Betsy died in 1841 and is buried in Carman Cemetery in Marion County. We have a photo of Betsy, probably one of our oldest family photos.

Alexander Shulse Father of Mary Ann Shulse, wife of James Henry B. Carman; Jo's third great-grandfather
Born: 18 August 1800, Rowan County, North Carolina
Died: 12 July 1887, Center, Ralls County, Missouri
Married: 1822 in Cape Girardeau County, Missouri, to Eleanor Whitledge
Buried: Salem Cemetery, Center, Missouri

Alexander was the son of Marcus Shulse (Shoults) Jr. and Christina Imbler of Salisbury, Rowan County, North Carolina. The year he was born, his family moved to Montgomery County, Kentucky. By 1822, Alexander was living in Cape Girardeau, Missouri, and married Eleanor Whitledge that year. Within two years, they moved to Center, Ralls County, Missouri, and their first daughter, Eliza, was born. Eleanor lived until 1866, and Alexander lived on the farm until his death in July 1887. He is buried in the Shulse family cemetery near Center, Missouri. Alexander and Eleanor had the following children:

- Eliza Christena 1825–1910
- Francis Jane 1827–1859
- Mary Ann 1828–1882
- William L. 1832–1905
- Mehitable "Hitty" 1835–1908
- Nancy C. 1838–1882
- Margaret 1839–1915
- Eleanor M. 1841–1921
- Nancy 1841–1921
- Lucy H. 1843–1908

Eleanor Whitledge Wife of Alexander Shulse, mother of Mary Ann, who was the wife of James Henry B. Carman.
Born: 20 November 1801, Bourbon, Kentucky
Died: 11 April 1866, Center, Ralls County, Missouri
Married: 1822 in Cape Girardeau, Missouri, to Alexander Shulse
Buried: Shulse family cemetery near Center, Missouri

Eleanor was the daughter of John Whitedge and Francis Overall of Prince William County, Virginia. By 1830, Eleanor and her parents had moved to Cape Girardeau, Missouri, where she met and married Alexander. Her parents also moved north to Perry, Ralls County, about ten miles from her and Alexander's farm. We believe Eleanor is buried in the Shulse family cemetery near Center, Missouri.

Henry Dilts Father of Albert G. Dilts; Jo's third great-grandfather
Born: 1767, Hunterdon County, New Jersey
Died: 17 March 1836, York, Dearborn County, Indiana
Married: 1785 in Fayette County, Pennsylvania, to Christena Harman
    Second marriage: 1831 in Dearborn County, Indiana, to Clarissa Hasty
Buried: Unknown location in Indiana

Henry was born in 1767 in New Jersey to Phillip Dilts and Mary Hoffman. By 1798 Henry and family, including his wife Christena Hoffman and mother and father, had moved from Springhill Township, Fayette County, Pennsylvania, to Wood County, Virginia. Wood County is now part of West Virginia. He probably had one of eight children by the time of this move.

He and Christena moved west to Dearborn County, Indiana, around 1817, where he remained until his death in 1836. His first wife, Christena, died prior to 1831, and he married Clarissa Hasty in 1831 in Dearborn County. He and Clarissa had no children. It was interesting to find that Henry died in 1836 only about four years after marriage to Clarissa. There was a subsequent court case in which Henry's son William fought in Dearborn courts to force settlement of his estate. The claim was that he was not married to Clarissa, but the marriage records did exist. From these documents came the proof of the names of Henry's children to include Albert G. discussed above. He owned a fairly large tract of land for the time period, and he died with a will. We can assume his second wife did not file probate proceedings until forced to do so.

Exploration of this family line was challenging until we found previous research done by professional researcher Darrell Conger a number of years ago. This work was useful in establishing the family moves from New Jersey to Pennsylvania, West Virginia, and on to Indiana. It is important to note that, as discussed earlier, the spelling of the family name varied over the years. We saw Diltz, Dietz, Dils, Dills, and finally Dilts.

Henry and Christena had the following ten children:
- Phillip 1736–1856
- Peter 1786–1881
- Anna Martin 1789–1846
- Mary Polly Riley 1797–1841
- Henry Jr. 1798–1866
- Jacob 1801–1868
- William 1803–1875
- Stokely 1806–1876
- Albert G. 1807–1880
- Jane Woley 1813–1835

We are uncertain of Henry's burial location; the kids probably could not afford a stone because of the court case expense (bad guess).

Christena Harmon First wife of Henry Dilts; Jo's third great-grandmother
Born: 1767, Rowan County, North Carolina
Died: Prior to 1831 in Dearborn County, Indiana
Married: 1785 in Fayette County, Pennsylvania
Buried: Unknown location

We have been unable to discover her parents or other family information.

Jenkins Henry Rownd Father of Nancy Rownd, wife of Albert G. Dilts; Jo's third great-
  grandfather
Born: 12 June 1791, Maryland
Died: 30 June 1875 in Dearborn County, Indiana
Married: 19 December 1815 in Snow Hill, Worcester County, Maryland, to Leah Savage
  Evans
Buried: Unknown location

Jenkins was the son of William Rownd Sr. and Martha Read of Snow Hill, Worcester
County, Maryland. He served in the Thirty-Seventh Regiment of the Maryland Militia
during the War of 1812. This would likely have been a ninety-day enlistment, and he
served as a private.

He married Leah Savage Evans on 19 December 1815 following the war, and their
first daughter, Nancy, was born in December 1816. Nancy later became the wife of Albert
G. Dilts, discussed above. By the time they married, her parents had moved to Dearborn
County, Indiana, which is where they probably met.

Jenkins and his family moved several times during their life. They moved to Fairfield,
Highland County, Ohio, by 1820, to Ripley County, Indiana, by 1825, and to Dearborn
County, Indiana, by 1830. Jenkins died in Dearborn County on 30 June 1875. The several
moves by his family might be attributed to the fact that (we believe) he served as a
postmaster in one or more of these locations. We also found records showing that he was
also a carpenter and later a cooper.

He and Leah had the following nine children:
  * Nancy 1816–1900
  * William H. 1818–1847
  * Elnor E. 1820–1900
  * Lewis 1820–1901
  * Sarah Samantha 1825–1887
  * Martha 1827–1827
  * Hezekiah J. 1828–?
  * Mary Jean 1831–1902
  * Harriet J. 1833–After 1875

Leah Ann Savage Evans Wife of Jenkins Henry Rownd; Jo's third great-grandmother
Born: 6 October 1794 at Snow Hill, Worcester County, Maryland
Died: After 1833
Married: 19 December 1815, Snow Hill, Worcester County, Maryland
Buried: Unknown location

Leah Ann was the daughter of Henry Evans Jr. and Sally Rice of Snow Hill, Worcester County, Maryland. Little is known of her family except her father probably came from Vermont and died in New York. She married Jenkins Henry Rownd in Snow Hill in 1815. Her death date is only a guess and was established by the birth year of her last child. Her burial location in unknown.

Alexander Cooper Baker Father of Ann Elizabeth Baker, wife of Henry Boren; Jo's third great-grandfather
Born: 1782 in Hartford County, Maryland
Died: 19 May 1860 in St. Louis, Missouri
Married: 1 March 1808 in Washington, Maryland, to Mary Webb
Buried: Bellefontaine Cemetery, St. Louis, Missouri

Alexander was the son of Maurice Baker and Mary Allender of Hartford County, Maryland. This is an old Maryland family that can be traced to the *Mayflower*. Maurice signed an oath of fidelity in 1778 in Maryland during the Revolutionary War, making him eligible for recognition as a Patriot of that war by the DAR. He was probably named after his grandfather Alexander Baker.

Alexander married Mary Poly Webb of Washington, Maryland, on 1 March 1808. Two of Alexander's brothers married sisters of Mary. After all ten children were born, they moved to Marion County, Missouri, near Hannibal, and operated a large farm there until 1860. Most of their children moved with them. Alexander died in 1860 in St. Louis, Missouri, and is buried in the Bellefontaine Cemetery there with his wife. Their children were:

- Morris Baker 1813–After 1850
- Mary Stover 1815–1851
- Anne Elizabeth Boren 1817–1880
- Rachel Heckart 1818–1850
- Thomas Alexander 1819–1854
- Catherine Anne Davis 1821–1890
- Louisa Mary 1823–?
- Pointon 1826–After 1850
- Benjamin Franklin 1829–After 1880
- Hiram Nicholas 1832–1891

We know that Anne is the daughter of Alexander and Mary Poly because we have Maryland birth records listing her birth to them. Additionally, the published *History of Tuscarawas County, Ohio* lists the children of her grandfather Maurice and his father, Alexander.

Alexander's farming operation in Marion County near Hannibal, from 1850 until his death in 1860, was a very large operation with stated valuation in 1860 as $22,000. His sons were employed by the farm as carpenters and coopers. We could find no evidence of slave ownership, which was common in Marion County in the Hannibal area then.

Mary Poly Webb Wife of Alexander Cooper Baker; Jo's third great-grandmother.
Born: 1786, Leitersburg, Washington County, Maryland
Died: 4 December 1859, St. Louis, Missouri
Married: 1 March 1808 in Washington, Maryland, to Alexander Cooper Baker
Buried: Bellefontaine Cemetery, St. Louis, Missouri

Mary was the daughter of William Webb III and Eleanor Charlton of Leitersburg, Washington County, Maryland. William was a Revolutionary War Patriot and served in the Continental Army, to be discussed later in this story. William and Eleanor were born in Maryland and spent their entire lives there, except for his military service. Eleanor's father, Arthur Carlton, was a very early settler in Maryland and owned and operated a tavern. Mary's sister Ann Phoebe married into the Key family of Francis Scott Key fame.

We have not proven that Mary Poly was the daughter of William Webb III. She was born and married in Leitersburg, Washington County, the lifetime residence of William III and his father, William Jr. The 1790 Washington County census shows one female child of the correct age group, but her name was not given. The census shows only one Webb family in that county in both the 1790 and 1800 census. We hope to find probate records or public reference to prove that relationship.

Thomas Burris Embree Father of Nancy Ann Embree, second wife of Davis Scott; Jo's third great-grandfather
Born: 1774, Orange County, Virginia
Died: September 1845, Middle Grove, Monroe County, Missouri
Married: 24 August 1796 in Clark County, Kentucky, to Elizabeth "Betsy" Duncan
Buried: Burris/Embree/Fox family cemetery, three-quarters of a mile west of Newman/Embree farm near the Monroe/Randolph county line

Thomas was born in Orange County, Virginia, to Joseph Embree and Mildred Burris. These families first moved from Virginia to Clark County, Kentucky, by 1793 and on to Missouri by 1818. This family included Thomas, his father, and several members of the Burris family.

Thomas served in the War if 1812 in Kentucky and lived in Madison County, Kentucky, after the war. We believe he did not move, but county lines did change as Kentucky was not yet a state, and smaller counties were formed from Clark County.

Their westward movement first stopped in Howard County, Missouri. In 1818, most of the soon-to-be state of Missouri west of St. Charles County was Howard County. By 1823, Thomas was soon on the move to Monroe County. We believe that his daughter Nancy Ann may have met Davis Scott in Howard County after the death of his first wife. They were married in 1828 in Howard County.

The Embrees, Burisses, and Foxes are recognized as the first settlers of Monroe County. Davis Scott soon followed deeper into Monroe County east of what was to be Paris, Missouri. These original Monroe County settlers are buried on the Burris/Embree/Fox land in Monroe County near Middle Grove.

We believe that Thomas and Betsy had fourteen children. This family is a study of the westward movement of Americans during the nineteenth century. Their children settled from Kentucky to Oregon within twenty-five years. They lost one son who died in Nebraska on his way to the California Gold Rush. One son moved to Oregon and was one of the first settlers in the Willamette Valley. He was successful in the California Gold Rush and later became a long-time Oregon farmer with a large family. We have the story of his travels to Oregon, and it is the stuff of legends. Two daughters also later settled in Oregon. One of the daughters married the territorial governor of Oregon. Their children were:

- Isham 1795–1872. Settled in Howard County
- Martillas 1796–1850. Died in Nebraska going to California
- Demarcus D. 1797–1845. Died in Madison, Missouri
- Lucinda Duncan Ford 1799–1875. Died in Polk, Oregon. Married governor of Oregon.
- Luvina Elkin 1802–1900. Died in Howard County
- Joseph 1804–1865. Died in Polk, Oregon
- Carey Duncan 1806–1900. Died in Polk, Oregon
- Mary Jane Cox 1807–1864. Died in Monroe County, Missouri
- Thomas 1808–1845. Died in Monroe County, Missouri
- Nancy Ann Scott 1807–1866. Married Davis Scott and died in Monroe County, Missouri
- Rosa Moss Brockman 1813–1893. Died in Chariton County, Missouri
- Milton Jackson 1815–1902. Died at Middle Grove, Missouri
- Sarah Mariah Ayres 1816–1845. Died in Saline County, Missouri
- Lewis Perry 1818–1885. Died in Chariton County, Missouri

Elizabeth "Betsy" Duncan Wife of Thomas Burris Embree; Jo's third great-grandmother
Born: 1776, Orange County, Virginia
Died: 1877, Monroe County, Missouri
Married: 24 August 1796, Clark County, Kentucky
Buried: Burris/Embree/Fox cemetery, Monroe County, Missouri

Betsy was the daughter of Joseph L. Duncan and Ann Nancy Stevens of Orange County, Virginia. Her father is a recognized DAR Patriot of the Revolutionary War, being so recognized for providing substantial support to the revolution. The Duncans moved to Clark County, Kentucky, following the revolution. That is likely where Betsy met and married Thomas Embree. Betsy lived to the age of one hundred years old and is buried in the same cemetery as her husband.

Her grandfather John Durron Duncan Jr. was also a Revolutionary War soldier of the Continental Line and will be discussed later.

George Allen Father of Melinda Allen, wife of Joseph Morris Crooks; Jo's third great-grandfather
Born: 1782 in Montgomery County, Kentucky
Died: September 1839 in Hancock County, Illinois
Married: 1806 in Kentucky to Barbara "Barbary" Myers
Buried: Cozad Cemetery in Hancock County, Illinois

Our George Allen research project is a lesson for researchers on why to always keep your mind open to the possibility of mistaken identity. This has been a nearly one-and-a half-year project in the collection of the various Allen family stories and documentation. Suffice to say we collected some book-worthy and colorful stories on the proposed father of George and his grandfather. We had the wrong man. There were two George Allens who settled in adjoining Kentucky counties and lived only a few miles apart—one in Floyd County and one in Montgomery County. Nonetheless, we are happy to say we have the right man here, be it a somewhat sad story.

George was the son of John Allen (1744–1804) and Hannah Tucker (1748–1794) of Montgomery County, Kentucky. George was born in Montgomery County and spent most of his life there. His relationship to John and Hannah is an unproven relationship. Research on this family line continues as this line continues to New England.

He married Barbary Myers in 1806 in Montgomery County. She was the daughter of Henry "Henrich" Myers, who had recently settled in Kentucky after moving from Fayette County, Pennsylvania. Henry was a Patriot of the Revolutionary War, and his story is told later in this book.

George joined the Kentucky militia as a lieutenant in the War of 1812. He served a ninety-day enlistment under the command of Lieutenant Colonel Barbee of the Kentucky Seventh Militia Regiment. He later received a 214-acre land grant for that service in 1832.

The 1810 and 1820 Kentucky census reports show George and his family living in Montgomery County. The 1830 census has them in Bath County. His 214-acre land grant of 1832 was in Bath County. Bath County was formed from Montgomery County in 1811. We are uncertain if he moved or the change was merely a county line change with the added Bath County.

George and Barbary had four children:
- Elizabeth "Betsy" Johnson 1807–1846. Died in Bath County, Kentucky
- William John 1809–1840. Died in Hancock County, Illinois
- Louisiana McCormick 1813–1884. Died in Montgomery County, Kentucky
- Melinda Crooks 1818–1880. Died in Monroe County, Missouri

We should note here that George had a sister named Melinda. Maybe he named his daughter after his sister.

George died in September 1839 in Hancock County, Illinois. The death location was puzzling, as his wife Barbary was living in Bath County, Kentucky. We found one researcher's explanation that stated he was attending a daughter's wedding and died during the visit. That was not difficult to disprove, as his daughter was married well before 1837 in Bath County. We eventually discovered his son, William, died in 1840 in Hancock County, only a few months after the death of George. We then found a billing for his casket in that location. The bill was for two caskets—one for George and one for William. George had ordered them both and paid a $7.00 deposit, leaving $13.00 due for both caskets. The balance was later charged to George's estate. We will speculate that William became ill and was being visited by his father. George also became ill and died within a month or so. William was only thirty-one when he died in 1840 and George only fifty-seven. We have their burial location as Cozad Cemetery in Hancock County, and we have a picture of the grave. The cause of their deaths is not known.

Barbara "Barbary" Myers Wife of George Allen
Born: 1784, Fayette County, Pennsylvania
Died: After 1850 in Bath County, Kentucky
Married: 1806 in Kentucky to George Allen
Buried: Unknown, but probably in Bath County, Kentucky

Barbary was born in Fayette County, Pennsylvania, to Henrich Henry Myers and Hannah Anna Miller. She was one of eighteen children in this large German family. Fayette County was a wild and dangerous county in an area contested by Virginia, Pennsylvania, the British, the French, and the Indians prior to the Revolutionary War. Henry, his brother, and their families were in the thick of this ruckus for a number of years. Both Henry and his brother served in the Virginia militia during the Revolutionary War. Virginia seemed to have a stronger presence in Fayette County at that time than did the colony of Pennsylvania. We cover this story in depth in our *Patriots* book. They suffered deprivation.

After the death of George, Barbary remained in Bath County. We find her living with her son-in-law Austin Johnson and his four children at the age of sixty-six. Barbary's daughter Elizabeth "Betsy," who had married Austin, died in 1846 at the age of thirty-nine. In 1850 Barbary was caring for her grandchildren. We are simply uncertain of her death date, but she probably remained in Bath County. Her daughters Malinda Allen Crooks and Louisiana Allen McCormick were also living nearby in Bath County. Malinda and her husband Joseph Crooks moved to Audrain County, Missouri, by 1860 via Hancock County, Illinois, and her other daughter Louisiana remained in Bath County and later Montgomery County, Kentucky.

We have the Kentucky birth records for Malinda to George and Barbary in Bath County. The daughter of Malinda and Joseph Crooks was Fanny Braden, who married DeMarcus Scott in Monroe County, Missouri. We presented the Joseph Crooks family story earlier in the book.

John Lewis Murphy Jr. Father of Fielding Murphy; Jo's third great-grandfather
Born: 1798, Jefferson County, Kentucky
Died: Before 1840
Married: 12 February 1816 in Shelby County, Kentucky, to Betsy Ashby
Buried: Unknown location

John was the son of John Murphey and Margaret Martin of Virginia. His father moved to Jefferson County around 1786 and was a farmer in that county for the remainder of his life. Father John and grandfather Lewis were both Revolutionary War Patriots and settled in Jefferson County, Kentucky, soon after the war.

John Lewis Jr. was, and remains, difficult to document. First, we have an abstract from the Scott family Bible showing John as the father of Fielding. Second, we have notes made by family member Lou Bridgeford Callis making that assertion. Lou was a close relative and was aware of the family history concerning the Murphys. Her research began with first-hand knowledge of that family over several generations. Her research has led to several DAR memberships over many years. More on Lou's knowledge of the Murphys below.

Back to John Lewis. He married into a historical family we have researched for years. It is worth the read in our *Patriots* book. He married Betsy Ashby on 12 February 1816 in Shelby County, Kentucky. Her father was Patriot Fielding Ashby. John Lewis and Betsy farmed in Jefferson County, Kentucky, and had four children:

- Lewis 1818–1869. Died in Monroe County, Missouri
- Rebecca Hess 1820–1903. Died in Monroe County, Missouri
- Matilda Elizabeth Oglesby Ashby. 1821-1903 Died in Monroe County, Missouri
- Fielding 1824–1900. Died in Monroe County, Missouri; Jo's second great-grandfather

Shelby County was formed from parts of Jefferson County in 1792, so that helps to explain John and Betsy's meeting, as the Ashbys owned land in both counties. We can find a son of father John Sr. in the Jefferson County census at an appropriate age. We can find a man the age of John Jr. in the 1820 Jefferson County census living with his father as well as a female the age of Betsy. We have John Jr.'s and Betsy's marriage records with Fielding Ashby's bond for the wedding in 1816. We have the 1830 Jefferson County census showing John Jr. with four children and a female of the age appropriate for Betsy. In this census, he was a neighbor of his father and he used the Jr. suffix on the census. There were no young people on his father's census report that year.

It is also worth noting that John Sr. owned slaves—at least sixteen—so he had a fairly large farming operation in Oldham County, which was then, and remains to be, the wealthiest county in Kentucky. This is Kentucky "Bluegrass Country." John Jr. did not own slaves in the 1830 census, but he likely was farming his father's land. If you are confused about how Oldham County came into the story, it was formed from parts of Jefferson and Shelby Counties in 1832. They never moved. John Jr. disappeared after the 1830 census, but we see Betsy spending the remainder of her life in Oldham County.

This mystery of John Murphy Jr. seems to be partially settled with Lou Bridgeford Callis's notes in which she said he left Oldham County bound for Monroe County, Missouri, with more than $300 in his possession and went missing after reaching the Mississippi River. He never made it to his destination and was never located. His son Fielding later made it to Monroe County by 1850, as did his brothers and sisters.

John Jr. was clearly headed to Monroe County to purchase land. Why would a man leave such a great environment as Oldham County? He stood to inherit his father's land. We don't know the answer to that obvious question, but consider this: You are from a family of self-made success stories. You have married into a family of Patriots from the Revolutionary and French and Indian War that had a rich history of helping start the American expansion to the west. I can imagine the rich stories told at family gatherings. See the chapter in our *Patriots* book entitled "Nothing There but Indians and Ashbys." John was clearly motivated to continue the family's adventure to the west. We believe Betsy would have understood.

We cannot document John's middle name of Lewis. His grandfather was Lewis as well as his first son and sons of later generations. Again, we find few documents about much of his life, but we have the right man here.

Betsy Ashby Wife of John Lewis Murphy Jr.; Jo's third great-grandmother
Born: 1792, Jefferson County, Kentucky
Died: 16 August 1855, Oldham County, Kentucky
Married: 12 February 1816 in Shelby County, Kentucky, to John Lewis Murphy
Buried: Probably in Ashby Cemetery in Oldham County

Betsy was born into the Ashby family and was the daughter of Fielding Ashby of Winchester, Frederick County, Virginia, and later Oldham County, Kentucky. Fielding was a Revolutionary War Patriot, as was his father and grandfather. We outline more than twenty Ashbys and their service to the nation during the Revolutionary War and French and Indian war. That story is part of American history and is included in our *Patriots* book. Betsy had seven brothers and sisters. This family made history. We will present her father, grandfather, and great-grandfather later in this story.

We find Betsy in the 1840 and 1850 census after the disappearance of John Jr. with children and a sister as a neighbor of her father. We believe she is buried in the Ashby family cemetery in Oldham County with her father and grandfather David Ashby. By the way, David was a personal bodyguard for George Washington.

Her father, Fielding, is Jo's Patriot for DAR membership.

Ellis Roney Father of Elizabeth Roney, wife of Fielding Murphy; Jo's third great-grandfather
Born: 1805, Washington County, Pennsylvania
Died: 1853, Oldham County, Kentucky
Married: 12 February 1823 to Maria Oglesby
Buried: Unknown location in Oldham County, Kentucky

Ellis is the son of Hercules Roney III and Margaret Buchanan of Washington County, Pennsylvania. This was a large family of German descent, with him having ten brothers and sisters. He was the next-to-youngest child. He was born three months after his father wrote his final will and was not named in that will, thus making proof of his lineage difficult, as the will was not updated prior to his father's death. We had elected to not include Hercules in the *Patriots* book because of that lack of evidence. Fortunately, we found records from the Scott family Bible retained by Richard Scott during his family research several years ago. That information proved the relationship. We have recently discovered additional proof of the relationship in the Oldham County court records. Ellis is definitely the son of Hercules III.

After the death of his father in 1812, Ellis moved to Shelby County, Kentucky, with his mother and several brothers and sisters. We believe that this move occurred soon after the death of Hercules. We see property transactions between the Roneys in Shelby County by 1815. An interesting side note is that we also found records between the Roneys and the Roberts family, who are members of the Adams/Raines lines. Ellis and Maria married on 12 February 1823, a year after the death of his mother.

By 1830, the Roneys lived in Oldham County, Kentucky. Why did they move? The fact is that they did not move, but the map moved. County lines were frequently changed in Kentucky in the early 1800s. The Roneys were a large, tight-knit family—we saw nieces living with uncles after the death of a father, and several land transactions between family members. Shelby County was much more peaceful than Fayette County, Pennsylvania.

Ellis and Maria had eight children:
- Elizabeth Murphy 1823–1882. She married Fielding Murphy
- John 1825–1881. Died in Monroe County, Missouri
- Joshua Everett 1825–1881. Died in Monroe County, Missouri
- John 1825–1881. Died in Monroe County, Missouri
- Mary E. Roney 1830–1900. Married a Roney and died in Kentucky
- Matilda Infield 1831–1918. Died in Oklahoma
- James S. 1834–1882. Died in Monroe County, Missouri
- Emma 1840–1858 (She may not have reached adulthood.)

Maria Oglesby Wife of Ellis Roney
Born: 1800, Jefferson County, Kentucky
Died: 1856, Iowa
Married: 12 February 1823 to Ellis Roney
Buried: Unknown location in Iowa

Maria was born in Jefferson County, Kentucky, to Jesse Oglesby and Celia Witt, originally of Amherst County, Virginia. Jesse was a Revolutionary War Patriot discussed in our *Patriots* book. Their move to Kentucky the year of Maria's birth was the result of a land grant. Celia's grandfather David was also a Patriot of the revolution.

We believe Maria died and is buried in Iowa. She may have moved there and died following the death of Ellis.

James Crooks IV Probable father of James Morris Crooks, who is the father of Fannie Braden Crooks Scott; Jo's third great-grandfather
Born: 16 April 1786 in Frederick County, Maryland
Died: 5 May 1813 at Fr. Meigs, Ohio
Married: 1809 in Montgomery County, Kentucky, to Agigal Frier
Buried: At Fort Meigs National Monument

James was the son of James Crooks III and Anne Braden of Maryland, Virginia, and later Bath County, Kentucky. The Crooks family arrived in New Jersey and moved to Loudoun County, Virginia. The family of James Crooks Jr., father of James III, moved and settled in Pennsylvania, Virginia, Kentucky, and later South Carolina. We have researched the entire family, but our study has centered on the Kentucky line.

James IV was born in Frederick County, Maryland, and moved to Loudoun County, Virginia, by 1788 with his family. By 1800, James was living in Nelson County, Kentucky, possibly with his brother Robert Braden. In 1809, he married Abigal Frier in Winchester, Clark County, Kentucky. By 1810, they had moved to Montgomery County, Kentucky. The 1810 census shows him in Montgomery County along with his brothers Uzal and John and their families. Bath County was divided from Montgomery County in 1811, so Bath County was the home of the Crooks family then.

He enlisted in the Kentucky militia as a private on 29 March 1813. His unit was the Thirteenth Kentucky Militia Regiment commanded by Colonel William Dudley. His company commander was Captain Joseph Clark. His unit soon received orders to march into the northwest territory to Fort Meigs, in what is now the state of Ohio. The fort was located on the Maumee River. The unit consisted of as many as 1,200 men at the start of the campaign. The regiment was to drive the British from Fort Meigs and destroy their cannons. The British had recently driven the American forces from the fort. They attacked on 5 May and nothing went well for them. Colonel Dudley was killed in the first few minutes of battle, but they did drive the British from the fort. The soldiers of the regiment then decided without orders to attack the Indians who had been firing on them from outside the fort as they attacked. They were all quickly captured by the Indians and British, who started them on a march to Fort Maumee as prisoners. The Indians continued to kill the Americans along the route until Chief Tecumseh intervened and stopped the bloodshed while the British just stood by watching. There were 150 soldiers killed in the march as well as over 650 killed at Fort Meigs. James was likely killed in the initial battle at Fort Meigs along with his regimental commander and company commander. He served one month and eight days and was paid $10.05 in advance upon enlistment. Only 150 men survived the battle out of the original 1,200. This was one of the bloodiest battles of the War of 1812.

We believe that son Joseph Morris was born in late 1813 or early 1814. James and Abigal may have had a son prior to Joseph Morris, as he is shown with a wife and son under ten in the 1810 Montgomery County census. He was likely born in Bath County, but his mother and father never moved because Bath County was formed from Montgomery County.

It is likely that James was buried on the grounds at Fort Meigs, which is now a national historic monument, although we believe no official listing of those killed in battle has been produced. His military records attest to his unit and date of death. It is also likely that none of those lost in this battle were ever buried. None were left to do so.

Chapter 8
Sixth Generation—Fourth Great-Grandparents

"Every man is a quotation from all his ancestors."
—Ralph Waldo Emerson

We should point out that in the following three chapters, some of the ancestors we highlight served in one capacity or another in support of the Revolutionary War, so we've placed this Colonial soldier symbol to the right of their name and personal information. Not everyone so annotated served in the military. We also recognize, as do the Daughters of the American Revolution and the Sons of the American Revolution, those who supported the revolution by selling goods and services, taking a fidelity oath, or serving on the various committees for safety or in a political office. It is not unusual to see the term "deprivation" used in connection with the families selling goods and services to the Revolutionary War units. Some of these families suffered true deprivation as a result of losing food and livestock to the cause. They were not reimbursed for several years, or ever. There were women who served in these important capacities, and they are finally being recognized for their important contributions to our nation. Our research continues in this regard. The wife of the following Patriot may well be documented as a Patriot in the future. Eve Catherine Painter, wife of Jacob Painter, is a good candidate. We expect there will be others.

Jacob Painter Father of George Washington Painter; Jo's fourth great-grandfather
Born: 1743, York, Pennsylvania
Died: 5 June 1824, Berkley County, Virginia
Married: First marriage: Unknown
    Second marriage: 1773 in Pennsylvania to Eve Catherine Seibert
Buried: German Lutheran Reformed Cemetery, Martinsburg, Berkley County, West Virginia

Jacob was the son of George Washington Painter II and Mary Magdalena Reinhart of Mosbach, Baden, Germany. They had moved to America by the time of Jacob's birth, and Jacob was probably born in York, Pennsylvania, very soon after their arrival. He had five brothers and sisters, including a brother named George Washington III. That is a repeated family given name.

He married Eve Catherine Seibert in 1773 in Chester County, Pennsylvania. Eve was probably not his first wife, as his son Jacob Jr. was born in 1759. Eve was only four years older than Jacob Jr.

Jacob joined the Pennsylvania Sixth Battalion Chester County Militia in 1778. This unit was reorganized once, and late in the war he was reassigned to another unit. We believe he served until the end of the war. This is an interesting unit with a wild story we explain in our *Patriots* book.

Following the war, Jacob moved with his wife and some of their children to Berkeley, Virginia, now West Virginia, where he lived until his death in 1824. His oldest son, Jacob Jr., remained in Pennsylvania and became a state representative and county judge. Jacob Jr. also ran for Congress but lost by seventeen votes.

Jacob and Eve had eight children, not counting Jacob Jr.:
- Mary Magdalene Mong 1776–1852. She died in Berkeley
- Margaret Ox 1776–1855. She died in Berkeley
- Catherine Walters 1778–1855. She died in Berkeley
- George Washington 1784–1853. He died in Florida, Missouri
- Eve Catherine Black 1789–1861. She died in Berkeley
- Elizabeth 1792–1838. She died in Berkeley and probably never married
- Sarah Sally Neff 1793–1838. She died in Berkeley
- John L. 1796–1879. He died in Berkeley

It is no surprise that children are named after other family members. The name of Jacob repeats itself over several Painter generations, as does the name George. Jacob's daughter Mary Magdalene was likely named after his mother. Daughter Eve was probably named after her mother.

We found that Jacob divorced Eve in 1800 in Martinsburg, Berkeley County, Virginia. Jacob wrote his last will in 1823 not long before his death, and he willed his real property to his wife Eve. We will not attempt to explain. He also recognizes sons Jacob Jr. and John and states he has other children not named. Those unnamed people were his six daughters.

Eve Catherine Seibert Second wife of Jacob Painter
Born: 1755, Berkeley James County, Virginia
Died: 6 April 1827, Berkeley James Virginia
Married: 1773 in Pennsylvania to Jacob Painter
Buried: Unknown location

We know very little about Eve. Her birthplace is in question, but we believe she and Jacob married in Chester County, Pennsylvania, and that she was his wife during the Revolutionary War and was the mother of eight of Jacob's children. Our research is pursuing the fact that she may have aided her husband while he served in the militia, and that act would qualify her as a female Patriot of the Revolutionary War. Several wives of the Pennsylvania Sixth Battalion did so. Research continues on this family and their stories. The term "camp follower" takes on a new twist in this instance.

John Smith Father of Sarah Ann Smith, wife of George Washington Painter; Jo's fourth great-grandfather
Born: 1762, Beverly, Essex County, Massachusetts
Died: 1798, Berkeley, James County, Virginia
Married: 3 August 1783 in Beverly, Essex County, Massachusetts, to Elizabeth Giles
Buried: Unknown location, probably in Berkeley

Little is known of John except that he married Elizabeth Giles in Beverly, Essex County, Massachusetts, on 3 August 1783, and that they had at least one child, Sarah Ann, who married George Washington Painter in Beverly prior to their move to Florida, Missouri. We believe it is likely that John served in the Minute Men or Essex County militia during the revolution, but there are simply too many Smith surnames to sort them all out. Research continues on this line.

Robert Cleveland Greening Jr. Father of Robert Greening II, who was father of Eleanor Greening, second wife of John M. Amos Painter; Jo's fourth great-grandfather
Born: 1764 in Albemarle, Virginia
Died: 13 October 1840 in Boone County, Missouri
Married: 12 April 1786 in Albemarle, Virginia, to Martha Patsy Crostwaite
Buried: Unknown location in Boone County, Missouri

Robert Jr. was the son of Robert Greening (1725–1789) and Sarah Dowell (1733–1794) of Albemarle, Virginia. Robert Jr.'s brothers James, John, and Nehemiah served in a Virginia regiment during the Revolutionary War. His marriage bond was guaranteed by his brother James. Brother James married Sarah Crosthwaite, sister of Martha.

He married Martha Patsy Crosthwaite on 12 April 1786 in Albemarle County. Thomas Jefferson was a neighbor of the Greenings for the first census of 1790 in Albemarle County. Robert and Martha moved to Clark County and are listed on the 1800 tax list for that county along with his brother James and again on the 1810 and 1820 census.

Robert, Martha, and Sarah moved from Kentucky to Boone County in 1827 after the death of James, Sarah's husband, in Kentucky. Sarah made a claim for a pension based on her husband's Revolutionary War service, and both Robert and Sarah testified to that service. The 1850 Boone County census slave schedule reflects that they were slaveholders even after the death of Robert Jr.

Much of the information on the Greening family of Virginia was provided by Donald A. Wise of Oklahoma. He provided an extensive list of references of the family history, much of which covers Robert's brothers and their Revolutionary War service.

Robert and Martha had the following eight children:

- Franky 1787–1867
- John 1789–1845. Died in Monroe County, MissouriRobert II 1794–1860. Died in Monroe County, Missouri, and is father of Eleanor
- Nancy 1798–1840Ann Louisa Donaldson. Lived in Monroe County, MissouriJames R. 1803–1864. Lived in Monroe County, Missouri
- Martha Patsy 1804–?
- Linsey 1806–1867. Lived in Kansas

Martha Patsy Crosthwaite Wife of Robert Greening Jr.
Born: 1726 in Albemarle County, Virginia
Died: 9 May 1853 in Boone County, Missouri
Married: 12 April 1786 in Albemarle County, Virginia
Buried: Possibly in Crosthwaite Cemetery in Boone County, Missouri

Martha was the daughter of Isaac Crostwaite (1726–1811) and Elizabeth Rippetoe (1743–1810) of Albemarle County, Virginia. Their name is sometimes spelled without the "e." A later spelling in Boone and Monroe Counties is "Crosswhite." She had nine brothers and sisters. Her brothers John, Thomas, and William also moved to Boone County and farmed there. There is a Crosthwaite Cemetery in Boone County in which several of the family members are buried. Martha may also be buried there.

Henry Carman Father of William B. Carman; Jo's fourth great-grandfather
Born: 1765, New York
Died: 1813, Westchester County, New York
Married: Unknown date to Elizabeth C. Kom
Buried: Scrub Oak Methodist Cemetery in Westchester County, New York

Henry is the son of William C. Carman and Jane Vanderhoof of New York City, New York. He joined the Westchester County militia as an ensign in one of two Drakes militia regiments for the Revolutionary War. The Drakes were brothers who each commanded a Westchester militia regiment. These were home guard units and did not see much action. Henry, unfortunately, was accidently wounded by a pistol discharge and given a medical discharge and disability. This injury eventually cost him the loss of his left arm and may have shortened his life. He died at the age of forty-eight.

Henry married Elizabeth C. Krom, and they had three children:

- John W. 1787-1866
- William B. 1791-1874. Died in Marion County, Missouri
- Charles—Unknown dates

Virgil E. and Emma Jo Painter Raines

We were able to confirm his birthplace and marriage to Elizabeth through the death certificate of son Charles.

As discussed above, we are unable to prove that William B. is the son of Henry. The research continues. We are working with a New York descendant of Henry for further proof.

John Johnston Father of Betsy Jaquess Johnston, wife of William B. Carman
Born: 25 December 1774, Culpepper County, Virginia
Died: 3 December 1827, St. Francois County, Missouri
Married: 4 February 1802 in Winchester, Clark County, Kentucky, to Francis Hawkins
Buried: Unknown location in Missouri

John is the son of Martin Johnston and Nancy Wright of Culpepper County, Virginia. His father, Martin, is a Revolutionary War Patriot covered in our *Patriots* book and discussed later in this study.

We know John is the son of Martin from a pension application made by Martin's wife Sarah, who presented a family Bible naming John as a son. Sarah later sold their land to their children, including John, for $1.00. John was born in Culpepper County, the same birth county as his dad.

He moved with his parents to Clark County, Kentucky, prior to 1800, likely due to a land grant received by his father. He married Francis Hawkins on 4 February 1802 in Winchester, Clark County, Kentucky. They had seven children, of which two daughters have connections to the Painter family. Daughter Catherine married Tandy Stribling, and their daughter Narcissa was the first wife of John M. "Amos" Painter. Their oldest daughter, Betsy Jaquess, married William B. Carman, whose granddaughter married John Thomas Painter, and another granddaughter married Robert Parker Painter. The Painters are certainly kin to John Johnston.

John became a Missouri explorer near the time of the Louisiana Purchase, but prior to Missouri's statehood in 1821. He managed to be awarded a Spanish land grant and lived in Missouri prior to the War of 1812, maybe as early as 1803. This grant was near St. Genevieve and the historic Murphy settlement. He returned to Kentucky, actually just across the Mississippi River, and enlisted in the Kentucky militia for ninety days during the War of 1812. That was the standard enlistment period for that war for militia units. Two of his daughters were born in Missouri prior to the war. To get these dates in perspective, John was most likely living in Missouri with his family when Lewis and Clark were exploring it. Seems like all they had to do was ask John about it. We have seen undocumented family stories in which he described his relationship with the various Indian tribes. He got along with all except the Osage, which he said he did not trust. The Murphy settlement near St. Genevieve requires more research to further document Johnston's activities in that area.

John and Francis had seven children:

- Betsy Jaquess*/Carman 1791–1841. Died in Marion County, Missouri
- Robert 1796–1846. Died in Reynolds, Missouri
- Elizabeth Copeland 1899–1837. Died in Ripley, Missouri
- Catherine Stribling 1806–1894. Died in Stoutsville, Missouri
- Reuban 1806–1856. Died in Reynolds, Missouri
- Celinda Copeland 1810–.After 1870 Died in Reynolds, Missouri
- Emmeline Mills 1817–1884. Died in Reynolds, Missouri

*Betsy first married Isaac Jaquess, who soon died in the War of 1812. She carried that name along with the Carman name the remainder of her life. We have a photo of her.

Francis Hawkins Wife of John Johnston
Born: 1776, Orange County, Virginia
Died: March 1850, St. Francois County, Missouri
Married: 4 February 1802 in Winchester, Clark County, Kentucky
Buried: Unknown location

Francis was the daughter of John Bennett Hawkins and Sarah Elizabeth Moulton of Orange County, Virginia. John was a Revolutionary War soldier who moved to Fayette County and later Scott County, Kentucky. This is an unproven relationship with research continuing. John Bennett and Sarah Elizabeth were married in Orange County, and we believe that Francis was born there.

Marcus Shoults Jr. Father of Alexander Shoults, whose daughter Mary Ann married James Henry B. Carman; Jo's fourth great-grandfather
Born: 1765, Salisbury, Rowan County, North Carolina
Died: 31 December 1836, Cape Girardeau, Missouri
Married: 1787 in North Carolina to Christina Imbler
Buried: Unknown location

Marcus is the son of Marcus Shoults Sr. and an unknown mother. He is shown in the Rowan County, North Carolina 1790 census as married. His father is also listed on that census. He may have lived in Kentucky for a few years before moving to Missouri. We know that Marcus Jr. moved to Cape Girardeau with son Alexander, discussed above, and that Alexander in mentioned in his will.

Christina Imbler Wife of Marcus Shoults Jr.
Born: 1769 in North Carolina
Died: 31 January 1830 in Cape Girardeau, Missouri
Married: 1787 in North Carolina to Marcus Shoults, Jr.
Buried: Unknown location

Christina was the daughter of John William Imbler (1740–1806) of Rowan County, North Carolina, originally Pennsylvania, and Margaret Mary Elgin (1740–1816).

John Whitledge Father of Eleanor Whitledge, wife of Alexander Shults; Jo's fourth great-grandfather
Born: 1770 in Prince William County, Virginia
Died: March 1854 in Perry, Missouri
Married: 6 March 1793 in Nelson County, Kentucky, to Francis Overall
Buried: Probably in Salem Cemetery in Ralls County, Missouri

John was the son of William Nathaniel Whitledge and an unknown mother of Prince William County, Virginia. This is an unproven relationship. Research continues. He married Frances Overall in Nelson County, Kentucky, on 6 March 1793. This is an unproven marriage.

John moved to Bourbon County, Kentucky, by 1801 for the birth of daughter Eleanor. By 1830, they had moved to Cape Girardeau, Missouri, where Eleanor met and married Alexander Shults. Both families moved to Ralls County near Perry, Missouri, by 1840. John died in late March 1854 near Perry and is probably buried in the Salem Cemetery in Ralls County where daughter Eleanor is buried.

Frances Overall Wife of John Whitledge
Born: 1764 in Prince William County, Virginia
Died: 1855 near Perry, Missouri, in Ralls County
Married: 6 March 1793 Nelson County, Kentucky
Buried: Ralls County, probably Salem Cemetery

Frances is the daughter of Lieutenant John Overall and an unknown mother of Prince William County, Virginia. This is an unproven relationship, and research continues.

Phillip Dilts Father of Henry Dilts; fourth great-grandfather of Jo
Born: 1742, Koln, Germany
Died: 17 March 1801, Wood, West Virginia
Married: 4 April 1764 in Hunterdon County, New Jersey, to Mary Hoffman
Buried: Unknown location

Phillip was the son of Heinrich Peter Dilts and Anna Maria Kaes of Amwell, Hunterdon County, New Jersey. He, like his father, was born in Kirchdorf, Rhineland, Prussia or Germany. He immigrated to New Jersey around 1720 and lived in a largely German community there. There is some question as to whether this Anna Kaes is his mother, or another lady also named Anna. We found considerable research on the Dilts family of this era and location. Phillip was one of about seventeen children. One of his brothers, Jacob, fought in the Revolutionary War.

We have found research linking Phillip to his son Henry, but more substantial evidence is needed to consider this relationship proven, but the given names we see seem to indicate some family connections. Peter's will does not mention his sons. We have found marriage records documenting his marriage to Mary Hoffman. We have found other marriage records for Mary that seem to say there may have been more than one lady of German descent with the same name living at Amwell, New Jersey, who married another Dilts. More research is in order.

William Rownd Sr. Father of Jenkins Henry Rownd; Jo's fourth great-grandfather
Born: 23 September 1722, Wilmington, Kent, England
Died: 1817 at Snow Hill, Worcester County, Maryland
Married: 1765 in Maryland to Martha Read
Buried: Unknown location

His family connection to son Jenkins Henry is likely, but unproven.

Maurice Baker Father of Alexander Baker, whose daughter Anne Elizabeth married Henry Boren; Jo's fourth great-grandfather
Born: 8 July 1748 in Baltimore County, Maryland
Died: 1830 in Washington County, Maryland
Married: 15 December 1777 in Washington County, Maryland, to Mary Elizabeth Allender
Buried: Unknown location, probably in Upper Antietam Hundred, Washington County, Maryland

He is the son of Alexander Baker and Zipporah Hilliard of Maryland. Church records prove this relationship. Alexander's marriage to Zipporah is also proven with church records. Maurice was probably named after his grandfather, who lived from 1675 to 1762. We found the names Maurice and Alexander used over several generations in this family line.

Maurice married Mary Elizabeth Allender on 15 December 1771 in Maryland. They spent the remainder of their lives in and around Washington County, with Maurice dying in 1830.

We found some family histories attributing military service to Maurice during the Revolutionary War, but we were not able to prove that was his service. We did, however, find that he took an oath of fidelity in 1778 in Washington County. That act would qualify him for Patriot status with the DAR for patriotic service. While that simple oath might seem unimportant, it was a matter of public record. This was a dangerous position for colonists to take, placing themselves and their families at substantial risk. Had the British won the war, it is fairly certain that those public records would have resulted in harsh treatment for those men who had taken the oath, along with their families. Some of them would have been hung. It also proved risky for the reason that British loyalists would submit them to harsh treatment during the war.

As with the DAR and SAR, we recognize Maurice as a Patriot and have included him in our book because of his patriotic service. Our research of Maryland militia units during the Revolutionary War has shown that those units sometimes did not keep complete records. Most of their militia records were not given to the National Archives following the war, and proof of service is time consuming. We continue that search.

Maurice and Mary Elizabeth had the following seven children:

- Maurice Jr. 1778–1860
- Nicholas 1780–1839
- Alexander Cooper 1782–1860
- Mary Webb 1786–1862
- John 1788–1854
- Richard 1790–1859
- Catherine 1794–1864

All these children's relationships to Maurice are proven. There may be one additional daughter.

We found claims that Maurice was descended from the first Jamestown, Virginia, settlers. We were unable to prove this fact, but we have ample documentation from church records, Anne Arundel County property, and marriage and probate records to establish this interesting family history. This family line was in America 150 years prior to the revolution. They made history. These are Maurice's ancestors:

Father of Maurice:	Alexander Baker 1705–1750
Mother:	Mary Elizabeth Allender 1760–1851
Father of Alexander:	Maurice Baker III 1675–1762
Wife of Alexander:	Zipporah Hilliard 1713–1782
Father of Maurice III:	Maurice Baker Jr. 1635–1700
Wife of Maurice III:	Elizabeth Hill Griniff 1635–1703
Father of Maurice Jr.:	Maurice Baker Sr. 1622–1660
Wife of Maurice Sr.:	Joan Greenfield 1620–1660
Father of Maurice Sr.:	Rev John Daniel Baker 1605–1654
Wife of John Daniel:	Priscilla Palmer 1610–1655

Maurice Baker Sr. was born in Moulton Parish, Northhamptonshire, England, and married Joan Greenfield prior to coming to the Virginia colony of Kent Isle. He died in 1660 in Kent Isle. We believe his parents were Rev. John Daniel Baker and Priscilla Palmer. John and Pricilla came to America a few years before their son Maurice Sr. and his wife, Joan. We have not proven the father-son relationship, but it is likely. We have seen claims that Priscilla survived an Indian massacre at Jamestown, but that is not proven.

Kent Isle is the largest island in Chesapeake Bay and has been a part of Queen Anne's County, Maryland, since the colonial era. It was first established as Kent Fort in 1631, making it the oldest settlement in Maryland and the third-oldest English settlement in the Americas following Jamestown and Plymouth, Massachusetts.

William Claiborne, a resident of Jamestown, founded a settlement on the island in August 1631. The island served as a trading station for trade with Indians. The colonies of Virginia and Maryland disputed the ownership of the island until the Revolutionary War, when it became part of the colony of Maryland.

We believe that Maurice Baker Sr. and Joan Greenfield arrived on the island in 1651. We have a ship manifest. By 1651, when they arrived, the Jamestown settlement was being abandoned and the settlers removed to the new colony capital of Williamsburg. The King had revoked the Jamestown corporate charter and established Williamsburg as the capital. The Bakers may have arrived in Williamsburg. Future research will involve search of colonial records for their stay in that settlement and their move to Kent Isle.

This Baker line is the second-oldest family line of the Raines/Painter lines following William Adams, who settled in Massachusetts in 1628. When we prove the Rev. John Baker and Priscilla connection to Maurice Baker Sr., it will be the oldest family line. It is probable that Rev. John Baker and Priscilla were at Jamestown before acquiring land elsewhere in the colony, so the Jamestown claim may have substance. His proposed father John arrived in 1621 after being deported from England for being convicted of a minor crime or being a non-conformist. As a minister, he was likely not preaching the approved gospel. We have the manifest of his arrival.

Mary Elizabeth Allender Wife of Maurice Baker
Born: 1760, Maryland
Died: 2 November 1851, Baltimore, Maryland
Married: 15 December 1777, Washington County, MarylandBuried: Forest Hill Cemetery, Charleston County, New Hampshire

Mary Elizabeth was the daughter of Nicholas Allender Jr. and Mary Day of Baltimore, Maryland. She married Maurice in 1777 in Maryland and spent the remainder of her life there. Records show that she is buried in New Hampshire after her death in Maryland. None of her known children lived in New Hampshire, so this is not easily explained.

William Webb III Father of Mary Webb, wife of Alexander Baker; Jo's fourth great-grandfather
Born: 11 May 1754, Washington County, Maryland
Died: 12 February 1807, Washington County, Maryland
Married: 1773 in Washington County, Maryland, to Eleanor Charlton
Buried: Webb Family Cemetery in Leitersburg, Washington County, Maryland

William was the son of William Webb Jr. and Isabella Charlton of Washington County, Maryland. He married Eleanor Charlton in 1773. Other than his time in the service, he spent his entire life in and around Washington County, Maryland. We have his birth and marriage records.

He served in the Maryland Seventh Regiment commanded by Colonel John Gunby, and with a company commanded by Captain Johnathan Morris. The unit was organized in March 1777 in Baltimore and Frederick Counties. It was assigned to the First Maryland Brigade and to the Continental Line and commanded by General Smallwood.

The regiment entered Valley Forge on May 1778 with 235 men. The had previously fought in engagements in the Philadelphia campaign and in New Jersey. Of the 235 assigned men that entered Valley Forge, only 131 were fit for duty. The unit needed a rest. History credits this regiment with successfully blocking the efforts of the British army from following George Washington after his being ejected from Long Island following the battle of Long Island. Had they caught up with the colonial army, the war might well have ended early. We believe that unit rosters for this unit during the Valley Forge period no longer exist, so we could not verify that William was there. His company commander is listed as present, so we will infer that William was also present as his service spans the Valley Forge winter.

Following the Valley Forge winter, the unit was assigned to the southern department in May 1780. It had already fought in the battles of Brandywine, Germantown, Monmouth, Camden, and Guilford Courthouse in North Carolina. We devoted a chapter to the Guilford Courthouse battle in our *Patriots* book.

The regiment was disbanded on 1 January 1783 at Annapolis; however, the personnel rosters of this unit have not completely survived. We found the final payment records for William as the unit was being disbanded. He was paid 86 pounds and 11 shillings. This is a substantial sum of money and represents his pay for the war. This was a tough battle-hardened unit that Generals Washington and Greene depended on to never retreat. They lived up to that reputation.

We did not find a pension request for William and did not expect to find one, as he died before Congress passed the pension act in 1819. His wife would have been eligible, but she also died prior to 1819.

We also found a fidelity oath taken by William in early 1777 prior to joining the army. This act alone would qualify him for DAR recognition as a Patriot.

William and Eleanor had the following five children:
- Elias 1776–1814
- Sarah 1783–?
- Mary Poly Baker 1786–1859. Married Alexander Baker
- Johnathan 1788–?
- Souvanna Cooper 1792–1882

About Mary Poly: We have been unable to prove that she is the daughter of William. She was born in Washington County, Maryland, following the war. She married Alexander Cooper Baker of Hartford County, Maryland, on 1 March 1808 in Washington County. We have an 1800 Washington County census with a child her age in the family. There was only one Webb family in that county in 1800.

Eleanor Charlton Wife of William Webb II
Born: 25 June 1748, All Saints Parish, Frederick, Maryland
Died: 10 March 1818, Washington County, Maryland
Married: 1773 in Washington County, Maryland, to William Webb II
Buried: Unknown location

Eleanor was the daughter of Arthur Charlton and Elenor Harrison of Frederick, Maryland. They were married on 14 July 1742 in Frederick. Her father died the year she was born. We found several Frederick County records mentioning Arthur in which he held political organization meetings at his house. We also found that his daughter Ann Phoebe married General Key, whose son was Francis Scott Key.

Her father, Arthur, died in 1771 at the age of forty-six.

Joseph Embree Father of Thomas Burris Embree, who was father to Nancy Ann, wife of Davis Scott; Jo's fourth great-grandfather
Born: 1727, Orange County, Virginia
Died: 18 November 1818 in Howard County, Missouri
Married: 24 September 1767 in Orange County, Virginia, to Mildred "Millie" Burris
Buried: Unknown location in Howard County

He was the son of John Embree and Elizabeth Woolfolk of Orange County, Virginia. We believe this was the second marriage for Joseph, as he had two children born before marriage to Millie.

Joseph was the senior member of this noted family of explorers. They were living in Kentucky by the time of the revolution. He, his son Thomas, and his family were settling in Howard County, Missouri, before the War of 1812 hostilities ended there. Both Joseph and his son Thomas served in the Kentucky militia during that war, but remember, the Indians in Missouri did not get the memo concerning the end of the war. It continued until 1818 there. Monroe County history credits the Ezra Fox, Thomas Embree, and Joseph Duncan families to be the first to settle in Monroe County after they left Howard County. Davis Scott was soon to follow.

Joseph had eleven children; the first two were with an unknown wife:

- John 1762–1852
- Francis 1762–1852
- Jacob 1766–1797
- William 1768–1797
- Nancy 1770–1821
- Thomas Burris 1774–1845
- Caleb 1776–1849
- Mary/Polly 1779–1796
- John 1781–1828
- Elizabeth 1783–1860
- Isham P. 1788–1871

Joseph died in 1818 in Howard County before his family moved twenty or so miles into Monroe County near Middle Grove.

Mildred "Millie" Burris Wife of Joseph Embree
Born: 1750 in Orange County, Virginia
Died: 25 July 1797 in Clark County, Kentucky
Married: 24 September 1767 in Orange County, Virginia
Buried: Unknown location in Clark County, Kentucky

Millie was the daughter of the Rev. Thomas Burris and Frances Tandy of Orange County, Virginia. They had previously lived near Norfolk, then in Caroline County, Virginia. We can assume Millie had a hard life with frontier living and raising eleven children, as she lived to be forty-seven years old and died before her family moved to Missouri.

Joseph L. Duncan Father of Elizabeth "Betsy" Duncan, who was wife of Thomas Burris Embree
Born: 1 January 1752 in Fauquier County, Virginia
Died: 25 March 1826 in Clark County, Kentucky
Married: 22 May 1772 in Orange County, Virginia, to Nancy Ann Stevens
Buried: Unknown location in Clark County

He is the son of Sergeant John Durron Duncan Jr. and Dinah Bradford of Orange County. Joseph, his father, and his grandfathers were Revolutionary War Patriots discussed in our *Patriots* book. Joseph received a land grant and a pension for his father's service in the Virginia militia. Joseph is recognized for patriotic service by the DAR and SAR for providing supplies to the Continental Army.

Following the war, he and his family moved to Clark County, Kentucky, by 1787. Their move was between 1785 and 1787. Joseph and Nancy had fourteen children, two of whom died in their youth:

- Sarah Montague Collins 1757–1822
- James 1775–1842
- Elizabeth "Betsy" Duncan 1776–1877
- Peggy Daniel 1777–1818
- Nancy Daniels 1779–Before 1845
- Charles 1781–1818
- Mary Stevens Daniel 1784–1872
- John 1785–1795
- Anthony Thomas 1787–?
- Carey 1787–1848
- Lewis 1789-1873
- Dianah Lampton 1795–1851
- Joseph Jr. 1796–1870
- Lucinda M. Smith 1799–1896

Joseph and Nancy's daughter Elizabeth "Betsy" married Thomas Burris Embree in Winchester, Clark County, in 1796. We have those marriage records. He became a War of 1812 veteran. They were among the early settlers to Howard County, Missouri, and soon moved to Monroe County, Missouri. That family is credited with being the first family to settle in Monroe County near the present-day village of Middle Grove. Their neighbor was Ezra Fox, also one of the first to settle there. They are buried in Burris-Embree-Fox Cemetery near the Monroe and Randolph county line near Middle Grove. Elizabeth lived to the age of 101 years old after having fourteen children and surviving hazardous living conditions in early Howard and Monroe Counties, Missouri.

All fourteen of their children moved to Missouri. Two soon moved to Oregon. Daughter Lucinda married the territorial governor of Oregon and Joseph soon ventured to California for the gold rush. He was very successful in that venture and returned to Oregon to farm, later becoming a state senator. Another son, Marthis, died in Nebraska en route to Oregon and was buried there. Their daughter Nancy Ann married Davis Scott of Howard County in 1828, and they soon moved to Monroe County east of Paris. They too are credited as being among the first Monroe County settlers. Davis and Nancy are the second great-grandparents of Emma Jo. We have their 1828 Howard County marriage and property records.

Davis and Nancy Ann sold their Howard County property by 1830 and purchased Monroe County land at the Palmyra land office. We believe they were completely moved by 1831, the year the city of Paris was incorporated. Among their children was DeMarcus Scott, Jo's great-grandfather. Davis Scott was a successful farmer, part owner of the Paris Bank, and probably a lawyer. Several of his sons became doctors.

Nancy Ann Stevens Wife of Joseph L. Duncan
Born: 22 September, Orange County, Virginia
Died: 12 November 1832 in Clark County, Kentucky
Married: 22 May 1772 in Orange County, Virginia, to Joseph L. Duncan
Buried: Unknown location in Clark County, Kentucky

Nancy was born in Orange County and was the daughter of John Stevens and Sarah Montague. The Stevenses were originally from Caroline County, but little else is known.

Henrich "Henry" Myers Father of Barbara "Barbary," wife of George Allen, who was father of Melinda Allen/Crooks; Jo's fourth great-grandfather
Born: 1756, Wurttemberg, Germany
Died: 1824, Montgomery County, Kentucky
Married: 1773 in Fayette County, Pennsylvania, to Hannah Anna Miller
Buried: Myers Cemetery in Jeffersonville, Montgomery County, Kentucky

Henry was son of Johann Ulrich Myer and Hannah Catherine Frick of Germany and later Pennsylvania. Henry arrived in Philadelphia at about the age of ten with his family, and they soon moved to the frontier in Fayette County, Pennsylvania, an area near the West Virginia/Maryland border.

Fayette County, Pennsylvania, was a border county with West Virginia and Maryland. During the Revolutionary War, Virginia claimed much of the land west of the mountains, including what is now West Virginia, Pennsylvania, and Ohio. This area was disputed until the federal government settled the dispute in favor of Pennsylvania and Westmoreland County. Fayette County was formed from Westmoreland County in 1783, so the county did not actually exist during the war; however, we found several references to the county dating prior to 1783. Fayette County was the center of the Whiskey Rebellion in 1793 that was quelled by then President George Washington.

Henry was a Revolutionary War Patriot who served as an ensign in the Monongahela regiment of western Pennsylvania. This was a bloody time in that part of the state, and the unit was led by a historic figure, Colonel Gadis. Henry was fortunate to have survived an expedition into western Pennsylvania late in the war when most of his regiment was killed or wounded. His regimental commander, Colonel Gadis, was later a central figure in the Whiskey Rebellion in western Pennsylvania.

We believe that Henry and Hannah had fifteen children. We questioned the fact that their mother, Hannah, born in 1756, was having children in the 1790s at over forty years of age, particularly Joseph and Aaron, born in 1793 and 1796. But they are all children of Henry and Hannah!

- Elizabeth Rachel Jenkins 1774–1837
- Jacob 1776–1866. Jacob fought in the War of 1812
- Hannah Kirk 1777–1853
- Daniel 1778–1826
- George 1780–?
- Johnathan 1782–1859
- Lewis 1782–1863
- Barbary 1784–1855. Married George Allen, Jo's fourth great-grandfather
- Henry Jr. 1785–1828
- Solomon 1788–1870
- Francis Frank 1789–1888
- Rebecca Overturf 1790–1833
- Lewis Myers 1782–1870
- Joseph 1793–1873
- Aaron 1796–1870

We know that Barbary was the daughter of Henry Myers from his estate papers and the 1850 census from Montgomery County, Kentucky. Her daughter Melinda married Joseph Morris Crooks, and their daughter Fannie Braden Crooks married DeMarcus Scott, Jo's great-grandfather of Monroe County, Missouri. Joseph Morris Crooks has been the subject of an extensive research project for the *Patriots* book. We believe his father was killed in the War of 1812 and that both his grandfather and great-grandfather were Revolutionary War Patriots.

John Murphy Sr. Father of John Murphy Jr.; Jo's fourth great-grandfather
Born: Circa 1764
Died: Before 1840
Married: 19 March 1790 in Jefferson County, Kentucky, to Margaret Martin
Buried: Possibly in Murphy Cemetery in Oldham County, Kentucky

John was the son of Lewis Murphy and an unknown mother of Virginia.

Lewis, who is discussed later in this story, married Anne Johnson in Jefferson County in 1800, so she was not the mother of John. Lewis died in 1803, three years after his arrival in Kentucky. As John Sr. was born around 1760, we must continue the search for his mother. The circa 1760 birth date is based on his age claim at his 1835 pension hearing.

Virgil E. and Emma Jo Painter Raines

John was a Patriot of the Revolutionary War. Lou Bridgeford Callis made that statement in her 1987 research of the family, so that was a good start to our research of John Murphy. He was one of nearly one hundred people with that name who served, and that was the difficult part. We quickly found John Murphy listed as a Revolutionary War pensioner of Jefferson County, Kentucky. Maybe that was him. That listing gave his age at the time he filed the claim as seventy-six in 1835. This listing also stated he was a Virginia line soldier. That narrowed down our search to a dozen or so Patriots.

We found that no person had used John Murphy as a Patriot for membership in either the DAR or SAR. That does not imply he is not a Patriot; it merely means no person has filed a membership application using that name. We did find that the SAR recognizes his service, but that is likely based on his pension application.

We eventually found his claim for a pension filed in 1835 in Jefferson County. This request was later approved, and the pension number is S-13998. His memory seemed fine, and he was able to make clear statements concerning his service. He was a member of the Illinois Brigade and a member of the Dragoons battalion. The Illinois Brigade was a Virginia line unit commanded by General John Rogers Clark. Clark was an older brother of William Clark of Lewis and Clark fame. I have researched that unit for years and suffice to say that they were tough, well-led men with a difficult mission in the Illinois territory. John was proud to be a member of that unit. He was a private that served for two combat-filled years. He was eligible for a land grant for his service. The land warrant number is 1015, dated 23 June 1783, but we found no records for such a Kentucky grant, so it is likely he quickly sold that warrant and got his start in Jefferson County, but that is speculation. Jefferson County was not a military land grant county.

As discussed above, John was a farmer with at least sixteen slaves in Jefferson/Oldham County. He is shown in the Kentucky 1800 tax list, as was his father, and on the Kentucky 1810, 1820, 1830, and 1840 census. We found no records after 1840. The Kentucky pension list states he died in 1840 in Jefferson County. Ownership of that number of slaves in Jefferson County indicates he owned a large farm for that region.

The Murphy family Bible establishes John Lewis Jr. as the father of Fielding Murphy. The Kentucky census reports of the early 1800s seem to support that claim. The Murphy connection to Jefferson/Oldham and Shelby Counties in Kentucky is well documented, and we have been unable to find other Murphys in those counties.

John married Margaret Martin in Jefferson County on 19 March 1790, and we have the marriage record. One son, John Lewis, and a daughter, Mary, have been found. John Lewis Jr. married Elizabeth "Betsy" Ashby in Shelby County on 12 February 1816. Betsy was the daughter of Patriot Fielding Ashby, discussed elsewhere in this book. John and Betsy had four children:

- Lewis 1818–1869
- Rebecca Hess 1820–1903
- Matilda Elizabeth Ashby 1821–1903
- Fielding 1824–1900; Jo's second great-grandfather

All four children settled in Monroe County, Missouri, and are buried there in Pleasant Hill Cemetery.

According to family legend, John Sr. left Shelby County headed for Monroe County, Missouri, with a large sum of money in his possession for the purpose of buying land there. He made it to the Mississippi River and was never heard from again. We are unsure of the date, except of it being before 1840. We find his wife Betsy in Shelby County living with her sister as a neighbor to her father, Fielding Ashby, for the 1840 census. She died there in 1855 and is buried in the Ashby family cemetery. Fielding Murphy, probably named after Fielding Ashby, is Jo's great-grandfather. The photo of him at his Missouri home is shown earlier in the book.

Fielding Ashby Father of Betsy, who married Fielding Murphy; Jo's fourth great-grandfather
Born: 1762, Frederick County, Virginia
Died: 17 October 1842, Oldham County, Kentucky
Married: 3 February 1790 in Jefferson County, Kentucky, to Rebecca Earickson
Buried: Ashby Cemetery, Floydsburg, Oldham County, Kentucky

Fielding was the son of David Ashby and Jane Isaacs of Frederick County, Virginia. Fielding, his father David, and his grandfather Captain Robert Ashby were Revolutionary War Patriots. This family story is extensive and a part of American history. We devote only a chapter to the family in our *Patriots* book, but it deserves more. The chapter in our book is titled "Nothing There but Indians and Ashbys." The chapter's opening sentence, " The Ashby family, the French and Indian War, Colonial Virginia history, George Washington, and the revolution are inextricable names and terms," says it all.

Fielding and Rebecca had the following children, and they are documented in his will:
- Elizabeth "Betsy" Murphy 1792–1855
- Jane 1794–1860
- James 1795–1851
- John 1796–1844
- Matilda Robertson 1797–1855
- Francis Wills 1798–1852
- Sydney 1802–1853
- Rebecca Ellis 1804–1864

We found land transactions between Fielding and his father, David, in Jefferson County. David had extensive land holdings in and around Jefferson County, some of which fell in Shelby County. We found a landmark court case in which Fielding was sued by a man that had previously sold land to David, who later sold it to Fielding. The basis for the claim was that the sale unintentionally included more land than described and that Fielding owed $40 per acre for the added land. The judge gave incorrect instructions to the jury, which quickly rendered a verdict in accordance with the given instructions. That case is said to still be used by Kentucky law schools as an example of the importance of judge

Virgil E. and Emma Jo Painter Raines

instructions to a jury. Fielding probably should have been forced to pay for the added land but won the case. We found records of David's purchase of one thousand acres, and this might have been what the case was about. He must have taken possession of more than the stated one thousand acres.

We found that a brother of David Ashby served in the French and Indian War as a colonel and received a large land grant in Kentucky County of Virginia. He spent three years in that area completing a survey of his land before returning to Virginia to fight in the revolution. It is likely that this land was responsible for David and Fielding's move to that region following the revolution. It was the best land in the colonies. Oldham County remains to be some of the best land in the United States.

Rebecca Earickson Wife of Fielding Ashby
Born: 1762, Kent Island, Queen Anne's County, Maryland
Died: 1842, Oldham County, Kentucky
Married: 3 February 1790, Oldham County, Kentucky
Buried: Ashby Cemetery in Oldham County

Rebecca was the daughter of Charles Earickson (1710–1772) and Elizabeth Wilson (1712–1787) of Kent Island, Queen Anne's County, Maryland. Her father died in 1772 prior to the Revolutionary War, and her mother and entire family moved to Kentucky following the war. She married Fielding Ashby after their arrival in Kentucky.

The spelling of their family name has seen several variations over the generations. The family was from Sweden. We have used the version used in the wills and marriage records of the family, but we realize the spelling most common today has changed.

Our early research of this family indicated that at least one of the brothers had served in the military during the revolution, but that has proved to not be the case. Her older brother Benjamin took an oath of fidelity in Anne Arundel County in 1778 but did not serve in the military.

Hercules Roney III Father of Ellis Roney; fourth great-grandfather of Jo
Born: 1750, Antrim, Ulster, Northern Ireland
Died: July 1812, West Finley, Washington County, Pennsylvania
Married: 1777, West Finley, Washington County, Pennsylvania, to Margaret Barnes
Buried: Unknown location in Washington County

Hercules III was the son of Hercules Roney Jr. and Elizabeth Mary Barnes of Antrim, Ulster, Northern Ireland. Hercules Jr., Mary, and family arrived in Philadelphia and soon moved to Bucks County, Pennsylvania, and spent the remainder of their lives in that county. The father of Hercules Jr. had been a surgeon in the Irish army. We have seen claims that Hercules II was born in Pennsylvania, but we have found several documents that seem to prove the Ireland birth.

Hercules III and brother James found jobs as surveyors in Pennsylvania and western Virginia and were given land grants in Washington County for their services. That is where they settled. Washington County was frontier "wild west" country prior to the revolution, and the Roneys lived a rough existence in that county with plenty of foes—Indian, British, and Tories. Hercules II served in a Pennsylvania regiment during the Revolutionary War and is covered extensively in our *Patriots* book. The DAR recognizes his military service as well as his patriotic service for the deprivation suffered by his family.

Hercules III died in Washington County and is buried in an unknown location there. He left a will naming his children, but we did not find the name of his son Ellis included. That will was written the year of Ellis's birth, prior to his birth. We had decided not to include him in the *Patriots* book for our inability to prove the connection to Ellis. We just recently found research records of Richard Scott from the 1980s in which he had records from the Scott family Bible. Those records documented that Ellis was in fact a son of Hercules II and that the will had just never been updated after the birth of Ellis.

The Roney family moved to Shelby County, Kentucky, following the death of Hercules II, and we have subsequently found court records establishing that father/son relationship. We also discovered court records in which the Roney family made land transactions with the Roberts family in Shelby County. The Roberts family are Raines/Adams family ancestors.

We believe Hercules and Margaret had ten children:

- James 1778–1842
- William 1781–1831
- John 1783–1831
- Mary Reed 1790–?
- Elizabeth Cooper 1794–1850
- Joseph 1796–1841
- James 1799–1869
- Hercules IV 1804–?
- Ellis 1805–1853. His daughter Elizabeth married Fielding Murphy, Jo's second great-grandfatherDaniel 1810–1847

His son Ellis married Maria Oglesby in Shelby County, and we will discuss her father Jesse next.

Jesse Oglesby Father of Mary Ann (Maria), who married Ellis Roney, whose daughter Elizabeth married Fielding Murphy; Jo's fourth great-grandfather
Born: 15 November 1763 in Goochland County, Virginia
Died: 1 October 1852 in Richmond, Madison County, Kentucky
Married: 15 September 1794 in Amherst County to Celia Witt
Buried: Paint Lick Cemetery, Garrard County, Kentucky

Jesse was born in 1763 in Goochland County, Virginia, to Jacob Oglesby Jr. and Ann Bailey. Some records show his birth county as Amherst County, but Goochland County was the parent county of Amherst, which was formed before his birth. His parents had extensive land holdings spread over what was to become three counties. His tombstone shows a birth date of 1761, but that is not likely correct based on his pension statements.

In 1728, Goochland County was formed as one of the original counties of the Virginia colony. It was formed from the Henrico Shire, and by 1744, Goochland was divided into several new counties. Among the new counties were Amherst, Nelson, and Albemarle, as well as others. We have found records of land ownership, probate, marriage, and other legal actions involving five generations of this family in all of these counties to include Henrico Shire. The original Goochland County stretched on both sides of the James River to the Blue Ridge Mountains. To accurately place a given family, one must first date the transaction and then relate it to the map in existence at that time. As we developed the stories of the Oglesby family from Dr. William Oglesby (tenth generation) through the generations to Jesse Oglesby (sixth generation), we have strived to place them in the county or counties as those locations existed at that time. In reality, they never wandered far from their roots near present-day Richmond until Jesse and Celia moved to Kentucky.

Jesse is a Revolutionary War Patriot and received a pension for that service. He first enlisted as a replacement for another individual, then re-enlisted after completing that service tour of ninety days. He served in the Continental Line and saw combat. His story is presented in our *Patriots* book.

He married Celila Witt on 15 September 1794 in Amherst County, Virginia, and had moved to Jefferson County, Kentucky, by 1800. His father and mother remained in Virginia, but his brother, sister, and several uncles moved to Christian County, Kentucky, as we will discuss later in this book.

This was a slaveholding family; however, we do not believe that Jesse was a slaveholder in Virginia. We did find one slave on an 1820 Kentucky slave census. The mystery of where and why one slave was eventually answered when we studied Celia's grandfather's will. She was left one slave in that will after his death in 1818. Her grandfather David Witt Sr. was a Revolutionary War Patriot who we will discuss later.

Jesse and Celila had nine children:
- Sarah B. 1794–1855
- Jacob 1798–1860
- David 1799–1850
- Mary Ann (Maria) 1800–1853
- Jane 1807–1850
- Malinda Callison 1810–1860
- Nancy 1812–1891
- John 1814–1895
- Jesse 1815–1886

All his children are named in his will. We first did not find Maria but later found that Maria was a nickname used by Mary Ann. Her marriage records to Ellis Roney use Maria. We later found her death records in Iowa, and the name Mary Ann was used. They were the same person.

Jesse was buried in Paint Lick Cemetery in Garrard County. We found two other family Patriots from the Raines line also buried in that cemetery.

Celia Witt Wife of Jesse Oglesby
Born: May 1779 in Amherst County, Virginia
Died: 3 March 1855 in Madison County, Kentucky
Married: 15 September 1794 in Amherst County
Buried: Paint Lick Cemetery

Celia was the daughter of David Witt Jr. and Salley Abney of Albemarle County, Virginia. David was born in Albemarle County, which was later divided into Nelson County. He was a plantation owner and had extensive land holdings as well as many slaves.

We know Celia was the daughter of David from her father's will. The fact that the slave mentioned in her grandfather's will is listed on Jesse and Celia's census report the same year confirms that connection. Her grandfather also named two of her daughters in this will and left them slaves. Her mother, Sally Abney, is of the well-known Abney family. More on them in the next chapters.

James Crooks III Father of James Crooks IV and grandfather of Joseph Morris Crooks; Jo's probable fourth great-grandfather
Born: 1745, New Jersey
Died: 1823, Bath County, Kentucky
Married: 4 August 1773 in New Jersey to Ann Braden
    Second marriage: 15 March 1787 in Virginia to Elizabeth Warford
Buried: Unknown location in Bath County, Kentucky

James was the son of James Alexander Crooks Jr. and Mary Clarinda West of New Jersey and later Virginia and Pennsylvania. James married Anne Braden in Sussex County, New Jersey, in 1773. James and Anne had the following children:
- Uzal 1774–1824. Died in Bath County, Kentucky
- Mary Elizabeth Davis. 1776-1848 Died in West Virginia
- Robert Braden 1780–1845. Died in Bath County, Kentucky
- Francis Weatherby 1781–1819. Died in Kentucky
- Margaret Cravens 1783–1811
- James IV 1786–1813. Probable father of Joseph Morris; died in battle

James and Elizabeth Warford (second wife) had the following children:

- Abraham 1788–1859. Died in Kentucky
- Nancy Moreland 1790–1870
- Job 1792–1819. Served in the War of 1812
- Hannah Barkley 1795–1840
- Rebecca Jones 1797–1847
- William 1800–1875. Died in Indiana
- Mary Truly 1804–1808. Died in youth
- John Truly 1807–1896. Died in Oregon. It was his granddaughter Rebecca Hoefer who provided the family Bible mentioned above.

We have the Bible records proving the names, birth and death dates, marriages, and locations of these children. We also have the marriage records for Anne Braden and Elizabeth Warford.

While James married Anne in New Jersey, he soon moved to Loudoun County, Virginia, where all fourteen children were born. Anne Braden died 13 May 1786 about thirty days after the birth of James IV.

James married Elizabeth Warford on 15 March 1787 in Loudoun County, Virginia. They had eight children as described above; all were born in Virginia except possibly John Truly. We find James and his wife and two older children still at home in the 1788 Loudoun County tax rolls. The DAR recognizes James as a Patriot for patriotic service as he paid the Virginia supply tax in 1783. We could not find evidence of military service during the revolution. We have not included him in our *Patriots* book due to the unproven family relationship. His son was certainly James IV, but as discussed earlier, we have not proven Joseph Morris's relationship to his proposed father James IV.

We believe that James and Elizabeth lived in Virginia until 1800, when we see him on the 1800 Nelson County tax records and on the 1820 census in Bath County. Interestingly, we see a male on this census the right age to be Joseph Morris Crooks. Did he help raise the fatherless Joseph?

Chapter 9
Seventh Generation—Fifth Great-Grandparents

"I don't know who my grandfather was. I am much more concerned to know what his grandson will be."

—Abraham Lincoln

A general note for this generation is that it, as with the previous generations, is incomplete. While we have possible ancestors in some instances, we will be cautious and list those with proven connections to the various family lines presented thus far. This process will hopefully continue in the years to come.

George Painter II Father of Jacob Painter; Jo's fifth great-grandfather
Born: 1712, Mosbach, Baden, Prussia
Died: 5 January 1784, York, Pennsylvania
Married: 12 May 1738, Saint Mary, St. Marylebone, London, England, to Mary Magdalena Reinhart
Buried: Unknown location in York, Pennsylvania

George was born in Germany and immigrated to the U.S. through England, as evidenced by his marriage to Mary in 1738. We know the names of his children by way of his will of 1784. We have seen the middle initial of "W" attributed to George, but we did not find proof of that name. His father's name was Hans Georg.

George and Mary had the following six children:

- Andrew 1740–?
- Valentine 1741–1784
- George W. III 1743–1811
- Jacob 1743–1824
- John 1745–1824
- Christina 1748–?

They spent the remainder of their lives in America living in Philadelphia. We found him the year of his death with a home and five horses. We could find no evidence of his line of work. His burial location is unknown.

Martin Johnston Father of John Johnston, who was father of Betsy Jaquess Carman; Jo's fifth great-grandfather
Born: 1 February 1758, Culpepper County, Virginia
Died: 3 July 1820, Winchester, Clark County, Kentucky
Married: 1779 in Virginia to Nancy Wright
Buried: Unknown location in Clark County, Kentucky

Martin was the son of William Johnston and Nancy Wright of Culpepper County, Virginia.

He joined the Virginia Third Regiment of the Continental Line as a private under the command of Captain John Thornton in 1776. The regiment was commanded by Colonel John Marshall at that time. He fought in the battle of Trenton and later served during the winter of 1778 at Valley Forge, Pennsylvania. He was discharged in February 1778 at Valley Forge. He filed for a pension in 1818 in Clark County, Kentucky, and it was approved. After his death later in 1820, his wife, Nancy, filed for a pension and it was also approved. When Nancy filed for the pension, she stated that he not only served two years in the Continental Line but had enlisted in the militia following the initial enlistment. She stated that he had served in the King's Mountain battle, which would have been in 1780. We could not find a record of that service. In fact, his son William was born in Clark County, Kentucky, the month of that battle. His service in the third regiment is well documented and recognized by both the DAR and SAR, not so for the alleged militia service in 1780.

We can speculate that Nancy's claim for the pension should not have been approved on his service prior to their marriage. That was the law. The claim for militia service after their marriage would seem to enhance her eligibility chances. The facts of this claim may be lost to history.

During Nancy's pension request, she and son William presented a family Bible that listed their children, including John. She later sold the land left by Martin to all their children, including John, for $1.00 each. That Bible listed John's birth date and marriage date to Francis Hawkins. That pension request was denied. As a matter of note, the law for eligibility was later changed in the 1830s to accommodate wives who were not married to Patriots during the war.

Son John's birth date of 1774, as shown in the family Bible, presents a question. Martin and Nancy did not marry until 1779 after his military service when Nancy was age seventeen. We can only speculate that Martin had previously married, but that marriage is not shown in the family Bible.

Martin and Nancy had the following children:
- John 1774–1827. Father of Betsy Jaquess Johnston
- William B. 1780–1855
- Francis 1783–1832
- George 1788–1888
- Cornelius 1801–?

John Embree Sr. Father of Joseph Embree, grandfather of Thomas Burris, who was father of Nancy Ann Embree/Scott; Jo's fifth great-grandfather
Born: 1710 in France
Died: 1790 in Orange County, Virginia
Married: 1730 to Nancy Woolfolk
Buried: Unknown location in Orange County, Virginia

John may have been born in France as he and two brothers transited from France to the colonies. He originally settled in Caroline County and became a cooper and later purchased a four-hundred-acre plantation in Orange County. He spent the remainder of his life on that plantation. He and Nancy had five children. In the early 1700s, the Virginia colony counties centered on Jamestown and fanned out westward. The early Orange County was west of Caroline County. Orange County was the "wild west." John brought workers with him from England who served apprenticeships with him in his business. These people were indentured servants whose transit to the colony was paid for by him, and they then served six or seven years working to pay for their freedom.

His plantation was left to his son John Jr. in 1790 along with the slaves. Other property was divided among the four remaining children who were named in the will. His final estate was probably large, and we found modern flow charts attempting to explain the disposition of the property. Their children were:

- Joseph 1727–1818. Early Missouri explorer. Died in Howard County, MO
- Joanna Robinson 1731–1790. Died in Louisa County, VA
- Judith Robinson 1742–1830. Died in Clark County, KY
- John 1742–1818. Early explorer in Lincoln County, KY
- Richard. Dates unknown. Little is known of him

The burial location of John is unknown.

John Durron Duncan Jr. Father of Joseph Duncan, whose daughter Elizabeth married Thomas Burris Embree; Jo's fifth great-grandfather
Born: 15 July 1727
Died: 6 November 1788 in Fauquier County, Virginia
Married: 1747 in Prince William County to Dinah Bradford
Buried: Unknown location in Fauquier County

John was the son of John Duncan Sr. and Willkey McClanahan of Prince William County, Virginia. His father is recognized for patriotic service during the Revolutionary War by the DAR. He sold supplies to the army. His middle name of Durron probably came from his grandmother, whose maiden name was Durron. His father's story will be presented in the eighth generation to follow.

John Jr. joined the Continental Army's Fourth/Eighth Virginia Regiments in 1777 as a sergeant under the command of Captain Thomas Berry and Colonel Thomas Marshall. This was a very active Revolutionary War unit with an extensive combat record. The unit was captured at the siege of Charleston, and the soldiers remained as prisoners until the end of the war. We believe that John had been discharged by the time of capture, as he was probably discharged in 1779. He died at the age of fifty-eight in 1788. We have researched several other soldiers of that regiment who were wounded and injured during service. They also did not live long lives. John and Dianah farmed on a farm near his father's land in Fauquier County. He died in Fauquier County the same year as his wife Dinah. They are buried in an unknown location. Their children were:

- John III, 1749–1833
- William 1750–1830. Served in the same regiment as his father and died in Culpepper County, Virginia
- Joseph Sr. 1752–1826. Jo's fourth great-grandfather, discussed below
- Rose Murphey 1756–1830
- Chloe Kirk 1762–1821
- Leanna 1764–1830
- Alamander 1766–1856 Served in the War of 1812

We know that John Jr. was the son of John because he was named in his father's will of 1788. John Jr., who died later that year, did not survive his father, who died in 1795.

His regimental commander at enlistment was Colonel Thomas Marshall. Colonel Marshall soon was discharged and returned to Fauquier County, and later, as an attorney, was the writer of John Duncan Sr.'s will. That story follows later in this project.

David Ashby Father of Fielding Ashby; Jo's fifth great-grandfather
Born: 1737, East bank, Shenandoah River, Frederick County, Virginia
Died: 1803, Shelby County, Kentucky
Married: Possibly 1761 Jane Isaacs
Buried: Ashby Cemetery in Oldham County, Kentucky

David is the son of Captain Robert R. Ashby and Dorothy Bayless of Frederick County, Virginia. As mentioned previously, the Ashby family has a rich history associated with colonial Virginia, the Shenandoah Valley, and George Washington.

We spent months of research linking David with his father Robert. David was not listed as a son in Robert's will. This is a large well-documented family, and we chose to be prudent in not making this connection unless properly proven. We found several historical records in which David was mentioned in the same paragraph as his father and brothers. Robert mentioned in his will that not all sons were included as they had received all he intended to give them. We found court records in which David and Robert testified together for various reasons. That does not prove the relationship. We found George Washington's account of visiting Robert's home in which David was mentioned with his alleged brothers. David was later in the Revolutionary War and selected as a personal bodyguard for the General. We have not been totally successful in proving this relationship in spite of these facts.

We have collaborated with a descendant of David and Fielding, and he is confident of this connection, and so are we. We believe David and his father, Robert, were possibly estranged. We found some debt problems in which David was involved in Virginia, so maybe those problems were the source, but it is only a guess. David's birth date is consistent with his brothers and sisters. In fact, we have proven that he cannot be a nephew of Robert. It was a large family, but he fits nowhere else in the Ashby family of Frederick County. David is a son of Robert.

David married Jane Isaacs possibly in 1761. We have not found those marriage records, but we believe this is the correct wife. Jane came from a family of Revolutionary War officers from Frederick County, and we find a wife with the name of Jane in later census records. We found an early Frederick County history showing that George Washington surveyed land belonging to Samuel Isaacs, father of Jane. David was almost certainly on that survey crew. Maybe that is how he met Jane. We have several George Washington documents showing David and his brothers and his dad, Robert, serving on his Frederick County survey crews.

We found records showing David and his wife, Jane, sold 115 acres of land to John Milton on 7 September 1784 in Frederick County.

We will not recount his war records in isolation from the Ashby family at large. We explored the family's history with regard to the early exploration of Virginia, the French and Indian War, and the revolution. We devoted just one chapter to that effort in our *Patriots* book, and it deserves more. They were Patriots.

David, Jane, and Fielding moved to Jefferson County, Kentucky, by fall 1784, and he died in Oldham County in 1803. He probably did not move, but Jefferson was divided into several counties, including Oldham and Shelby.

We can link David to son Fielding from a property transaction and subsequent court records in Oldham County. David gave him his land, and the person who originally sold the land to David brought a lawsuit years later claiming he sold too much land to David and wanted more money. Interesting case in itself, but it also proves the kinship. David is buried in the Ashby family cemetery in Oldham County.

Lewis Murphey Father of John Lewis Murphy, who was father of Fielding Murphy; Jo's fifth great-grandfather
Born: 1740 in Virginia
Died: 1803 in Jefferson County, Kentucky
Married: 10 July 1800 in Jefferson County, Kentucky, to Anne Johnson
Buried: Unknown location in Jefferson County, Kentucky

We believe that Lewis was previously married in Virginia, as he was sixty years old at the time of this second marriage. His one known son, John Sr., was born in Virginia around 1760.

Lewis was a Revolutionary War Patriot serving in the Virginia Third Regiment, Continental Line, under Colonel John Marshall. He was a documented Valley Forge survivor in a regiment with a battle-filled history.

This family history was slow to unravel until we discovered the added "e" to the name. Some of Lewis's records have that "e" and some do not. That addition had confounded the research until discovered. We see both Lewis and his son John Lewis living in Jefferson County, Kentucky, on the 1800 tax list. Lewis did not live long enough to file for military pension.

David Witt Jr. Father of Celia Witt, who was the wife of Jesse Oglesby; Jo's fifth great-grandfather
Born: 1750 in Albemarle County, Virginia
Died: 28 August 1818 in Nelson, Virginia
Married: 1770 in Albemarle County, Virginia, to Sally Abney
Buried: Nellysford, Nelson County, Virginia, in Witt Family Cemetery

David Jr. was the son of David Witt Sr. and Sarah "Sally" Harbour of Albemarle County, Virginia. His father was a large land owner in the original Goochland County, which was later divided, forming Albemarle, Nelson, and several other counties. He owned land in Goochland, Albemarle, and Nelson Counties. We found several land transactions in which he bought and sold land to his wife's family. David Sr. was a tobacco grower and owned slaves, which we see being willed to his children in his estate. His will names David Jr. as a son.

The colonial Witt family were French Huguenot refugees awarded land grants by the King. Goochland County was the center of their settlement, which borders both sides of the James River in central Virginia. They settled there in 1700 and 1701. David Witt Sr.'s father, John William, received a large grant. David Sr. grew those holdings as did David Jr. Tobacco was the principle crop prior to the revolution, and slaves were the labor market. Tobacco prices fell after the revolution, and other crops became necessary.

David Jr. married Sally Abney in 1770 in Albemarle County. We have documented that marriage. David and Sally had the following eight children, all documented by his will:
- Dennett Abney 1771–1840
- Ann Sparks Fitzpatrick 1772–1850
- Cecila Oglesby 1779–1855. Emma Jo's fourth great-grandmother
- Malinda Linney Wade 1780–1860
- William 1780–1836
- Candice Dicey Hamlett 1781–1830
- Burgess Witt 1783–1872
- David III 1785–1844

David died on 28 August 1818 in Nelson County and is buried in the Witt Family cemetery in Nelson county, Virginia.

We have previously represented David Jr. as a Revolutionary War Patriot based on his signing an oath of allegiance in August 1777 in Henry County, Virginia. The DAR recognizes that oath and has attributed it to David Jr. We are not convinced David Jr. was in Henry County in 1777, and we no longer represent him thusly. Additionally, David Jr. was not old enough in 1777 to sign an oath. DAR records also reflect he sold supplies to the military as well as signing the oath. His father was the Patriot. We explain this change later in the book with the life of David Sr.

Sarah "Sally" Abney Wife of David Witt Jr.
Born: 14 March 1759 in Albemarle County, Virginia
Died: 18 January 1816 in Nelson County, Virginia
Married: 1770 in Albemarle County, Virginia, to David Witt Jr.
Buried: Nellysford, Nelson County, Virginia, in Witt Family Cemetery

Sarah was born in Halifax County, Virginia, to Dannett II and Cassandra Abney. She married David in 1750 in Albemarle County and is buried in Nelson County. Her family had large land holdings in Virginia but moved to South Carolina prior to the revolution. Her family ancestors had impressive British royal connections. See this in the next chapter.

Jacob Oglesby Jr. Father of Jesse Oglesby; Jo's fifth great-grandfather
Born: 1736 in Goochland County, Virginia
Died: January 1813 in Albemarle County, Virginia
Married: 14 February 1760 in Goochland County, Virginia, to Ann Bailey (1740–1780)
        Second marriage: 1780 to Mildred Martin (1741–1827)
Buried: Unknown location

Jacob Jr. was born in 1736 to Jacob Oglesby Sr. (1709–1780) and Constance Perkins (1709–1769) in Goochland County, Virginia. There is some debate concerning the family name of his wife, Constance. The family name of Perkins can be questioned, as the marriage records we have found merely show her given name as Constance. Some researchers maintain her family name was Christian. What seems to be certain is that they were married in 1726 in Goochland County. The relationships of the Oglesby family, Richard, son Jacob Sr., Jacob Jr., and Jesse, are proven by the Oglesby family Bible located in Missouri, as well as by marriage, probate, and census records mentioned elsewhere.

Father and son and grandfather were farmers and plantation owners in Goochland and Albemarle Counties of Virginia. As a matter of note, Albemarle County was formed from parts of Goochland and other counties in 1776. The father of Jacob Sr. was Richard, who had been a large landowner who married a lady who herself was a large landowner. Their crops consisted mainly of tobacco and hemp. Jacob Jr. served as a tobacco inspector for his county for several years. There was a tobacco warehouse belonging to the county, and the inspector job was a public appointed position that he held for several years. This warehouse had belonged to family who moved to Kentucky, and the county continued its operation in support of the local tobacco production. We could not document the size of Jacob Jr.'s plantation, but his land holdings may not have been as large as those of his father or grandfather. We found records of land sales he made to other family members, and these sales were for modest-sized farms of two hundred acres.

We found a Virginia 1780 reconstructed census showing Jacob owned four slaves that year. The 1800 federal census shows zero slaves, but given his age, perhaps his slaves had been sold or passed on to his sons. We are speculating that, prior to 1780, it was not practical to own slaves in Albemarle County due to the fact that it was a dangerous county because of Indian unrest. His sons who remained in Virginia owned slaves and those sons who moved to Kentucky did not take slaves to the county of Kentucky. It is a well-established fact that Thomas Jefferson held slaves in this county, but we believe it was well after the 1760s. As discussed earlier in the book, son Jesse owned a slave in Kentucky, but his wife Celia inherited that slave from her grandfather of Virginia.

Jacob Jr. married Ann Bailey in Goochland County on 14 February 1760, a fact supported by the above family Bible and Virginia marriage records. Ann died in 1780 at the age of forty after eight children were born. They were:

- Thomas 1761–1840. Died in Christian County, KentuckyJesse 1763–1852. Jo's fourth great-grandfather. Died in Madison County, KentuckyJacob 1764–1817. Died in Virginia
- Constant 1765–1840. Died in Christian County, KentuckyPleasant 1766–1847. Died in Cooper County, MissouriSusannah Sukey 1770–1814. Died in Christian County, KYJohn 1775–1802. Died in VirginiaMartha "Patsy" Dinsmore 1778–1868. Died in Indiana

He married Mildred "Miley" Martin (1741–1827) in 1780 in Campbell, Virginia. Miley had been married twice before, with nine children from her first marriage to Micajah Clark Jr. Her father was Captain Thomas Martin Sr., who had served in the Revolutionary War. Jacob Jr. and Miley had five children, which might serve to explain the lack of need for large slave holdings: nine children by her first marriage plus five of this marriage and eight of his first marriage. Their children by this marriage were:

- Mary Christian Estes 1780–1838. Died in Lincoln County, Missouri
- Elizabeth Whitney Fagg 1782–1851. Died in Pike County, Missouri
- Martha Patsy Cox 1783–1826. Died in Cumberland, Kentucky
- Pleasant 1789–? Died in Saline County, Illinois
- James 1794–1822 Died possibly in Christian County, Kentucky

We found no records of Jacob Jr.'s military service, but it is probable that he served in the local militia in 1758. Most free men were expected to participate in the Albemarle militia for the purpose of protection from the Indian population. The French and Indian

War in 1756 had left the area in a state of unrest. We have searched the various lists of militia members in that county and were unable to find his name, but these lists are incomplete. During our research of the Ashby family of Virginia we found that Albemarle County was frontier during the French and Indian War. Thomas Ashby commanded Fort Ashby nearby. His job was to provide security to the area. He did a fair job at that task, but he needed quite a bit of supervision form his commander, Colonel George Washington. We also found that Jacob was serving as a county constable in 1768.

Jacob Jr. is credited for patriotic service during the Revolutionary War for several acts:

1. He served on a jury for the purpose of inquiry into property owned by loyalists, loyalists ranked directly below Indians in popularity. Their land was subject to seizure by the courts.
3. Following the war in 1782, he made a claim and was reimbursed for a gun that was impressed by the militia, also for grain and meals and bacon for the militia. His claim was approved.
5. He signed the Albemarle County Declaration of Independence in 1779. This act has resulted in the DAR recognizing his patriotic service. We also noticed a fellow Albemarle County resident signing this document. His name was Thomas Jefferson, a colonel in the county militia.

Chapter 10
Eighth Generation—Sixth Great-Grandparents

"In all of us there is a hunger, marrow deep, to know our heritage— to know who we are and where we came from. Without this enriching knowledge, there is a hollow yearning. No matter what our attainments in life, there is still a vacuum, an emptiness, and the most disquieting loneliness."

—Alex Haley, Roots

John Durron Duncan Sr. Father of Sergeant John Duncan Jr.; Jo's sixth great-grandfather
Born: 15 July 1715 in Fauquier County, Virginia
Died: 4 April 1795 in Fauquier County, Virginia
Married: 1731 to Willkey McClennan
Buried: Unknown location in Fauquier County, Virginia

John was the son of Marshall Duncan and Mary Ann Durron. We believe his middle name was from his mother's maiden name.

John was a plantation owner in Fauquier County. We found his offer to the governor of Virginia in which he offered land in 1759 to the colony for the purpose of establishing the Fauquier County courthouse. His offer was refused, and Governor Dinwiddie accepted the offer of neighbor Richard Henry Lee for the needed property. This Richard Henry Lee is a Patriot of the Raines line featured in our *Patriots* book; John Marshall Sr. was also a neighbor and close friend. John Marshall Sr. was the father of Supreme Court Justice John Marshall. We also found that John Marshall Sr. wrote the last will and testament of John Duncan Sr. John lists John Jr. in his will, but John Jr. was dead by the time this will was probated.

While John did not fight during the revolution, we found that he is recognized for patriotic service for selling goods and services to the Virginia line units. Both the DAR and SAR recognize him for that service. Patriot Robert Ashby, whose story is featured later in this chapter, also sold supplies to the Virginia line units in Fauquier County. They were neighbors.

David Witt Sr. Father of David Witt Jr.; Jo's sixth great-grandfather
Born: 11 April 1720, Goochland County, Virginia
Died: 27 June 1808, Henry County, Virginia
Married: 1744 in Amherst County to Sarah "Sally" Harbour
Buried: Possibly in Witt Family Cemetery in Patrick County

David was the son of John William Guillaume Witt, who was born in France and arrived in Virginia in 1695 or 1696.

Records show his father received land grants from the king in Goochland and Amherst Counties and that he bought, traded, and sold land in several counties. He married Sarah "Sally" Harbour in Amherst County in 1744. She may have been a first or second cousin. He grew tobacco and held several slaves that we see being left to his children in his probate records.

We find him and wife Sarah "Sally" in Henry County, Virginia, by 1776, where he signed a fidelity oath to the colony as well as selling supplies to the Virginia forces during the war. They had moved to Henry County on the southern border of Virginia and northern border of North Carolina. Patrick County was divided into Henry and Patrick Counties by 1800. His estate was probated in Patrick County after his death in 1808. He had slaves, which he left to his children. He is buried in Henry County, as is his wife. His will names his wife, Sally, and their children. This seems to settle his death county and that he is a Patriot because of his patriotic activities.

We did not fully understand his presence in southern Virginia by the time of the revolution. We have since found other Witts also living in Henry County and believe them to be brothers and nephews. His brother Benjamin served in the Virginia House of Burgess, and it is speculation that David Sr. received a Virginia land grant there.

David and Sally had the following children:
- Nannah 1747–1850
- David Jr. 1750–1818
- Martha Mildred 1754–1826
- John 1755–1826
- William 1760–1840
- Sylvanus 1761–1855
- Joel 1763–?
- Elizabeth Dillion 1765–1808
- Sarah Belleropan 1772–1850

Sarah "Sally" Harbour Wife of David Witt Sr.
Born: 1732 in Hanover County, Virginia
Died: 1814 in Henry County, Virginia
Married: 1744 in Albemarle County, Virginia, to David Witt Sr.
Buried: Witt Family Cemetery in Henry County, Virginia

Sally was the daughter of Thomas Harbour Sr. and Sarah "Sally" Witt of Hanover County, Virginia. Her mother was a Witt family member, so we can assume that there was a cousin relationship between her mother and her husband David Witt.

The Harbours became large landowners in Goochland County, and we have found several land transactions between the Harbours and Witts in Virginia.

Captain Robert Ashby Father of David Ashby; Jo's sixth great-grandfather
Born: 1710, Yew Hill, Delaplaine, Fauquier County, Virginia
Died: 27 February 1792 in Delaplaine, Fauquier County
Married: 11 May 1735 to Dorthy Baylis
        Second marriage: 28 April 1783 to Catherine Combs
Buried: Fauquier County, Virginia

Robert was the son of Captain Thomas Edward Ashby Sr. and Rosanna "Rose" Berry of Fauquier County, Virginia. He married Dorthy Baylis in 1735. His first wife was a problem. George Washington was not a fan of her and documented his displeasure with her in a letter to Robert. Robert was also a problem to Washington, but he continued to command and remained a close friend of Washington throughout their lives. They were friends and friends sometimes tolerate friends.

We present the Ashby family in depth in our *Patriots* book and will not repeat those intriguing stories here. He and his father, brothers, and son David served as chain bearers and markers for George while he was surveying western Virginia prior to the French and Indian War. He received land grants for his survey work and his service during the war.

Robert operated a tavern and hotel named the Yew Hill Tavern near the Shenandoah River for several years. It was the best hotel in the area, because it was likely the only hotel in Fauquier County. He boarded horses and people, but not in the same rooms. His experience with serving large quantities of liquor (we have seen the records) may have served him well during the French and Indian War. Interesting story.

Robert was a company commander for George Washington in the Colonial Virginia First Regiment during the French and Indian War. As the name of the war might indicate, the colonial army faced as many challenges from the various Indian tribes located west of the Alleghenies as they did with the French. Robert was probably better at dealing with the former than the latter. Remember, we named a chapter in the *Patriots* book "Nothing There but Indians and Ashbys," so that speaks of their relationship. Then Colonel Washington should have taken Robert out of command for his activities, but he was needed for that particular job. Robert was too old for the revolution, but he is recognized by the DAR for patriotic service due to his sale of supplies to the Virginia line and militia units.

Robert and Dorthy had ten children. This list reads like a "Who's Who" for the French and Indian War and for the Revolutionary War. Equally impressive is the list of over forty uncles and cousins serving in those conflicts. The family gave much.

Those children were:
- William 1735–1773
- David 1737–1803
- Robert 1738–1780
- John 1740–1815
- Capt. Nimrod 1742–1764
- Mary "Molly" 1743–1799
- Benjamin 1744–1790
- Thomas 1747–1790
- Winnifred 1748–1790
- Ann 1751–1807

Robert's father, Captain Thomas Edward Ashby Sr. (1682–1752), was born in England, came to America, and first owned land that is now part of the marines' military base Quantico in eastern Virginia. He later moved to what was to become Fauquier County and operated a ferry over the Shenandoah River. This was frontier, and his holdings straddled a strategically important piece of property—the pass into the Shenandoah Valley in western Virginia. The gap was and remains named the Ashby Gap. Thomas was a militia captain prior to the French and Indian War and was a noted Indian fighter.

Dannett Abney III Father of Sarah "Sally" Abney; Jo's sixth great-grandfather
Born: 1730 in Virginia
Died: 30 December 1809 in Ninety Six, Greenwood County, South Carolina
Married: 1752 in Virginia to Cassandra Abney
Buried: Nathaniel Abney Cemetery in Saluda County, South Carolina

Dannett was the son of Dannett Abney Jr. of Virginia. The family can trace their presence in Virginia to prior to 1700, when they arrived from England. He and his father and grandfather Dannett Sr. had very large land holdings in Virginia. Their land holdings are documented more accurately than the family members.

Dannett moved to Saluda County, South Carolina, prior to the Revolutionary War and before selling his Virginia land holdings. Several other family members moved at about the same time. They had extensive land holdings on either side of the Saluda River. We found several grants in his name totaling nearly one thousand acres. There were several others of the Abney family also owning land on the Saluda River, and we believe Dennett's land was located on a tributary of that river.

While we have seen claims that he was killed in the Revolutionary War in 1782 while serving as an officer, we cannot confirm that claim, and we reject it. It may have been a relative by the same name. He lived until 1809.

Dannett is buried in the Nathaniel Abney Cemetery in Saluda County. We believe that Nathaniel was probably the senior family member of this line of South Carolina Abneys and that he was an uncle of this Dannett. Nathaniel was a doctor and served in the Revolutionary War is South Carolina as a captain. There was clearly a second Dannett Abney born in the early 1750s who was a son of Nathaniel. This Dannett was likely the Dannett killed during the Revolutionary War by a Tory officer. His death can better be described as a murder than a combat death. He was killed at home with his family present.

His death location of Ninety Six, Greenwood County, may seem unusual, but the number was simply the longitudinal line of this location. It was a common locational description in South Carolina in the colonial period.

We find his daughter Sarah "Sally" listed in his will. Sarah had remained in Virginia and married Davie Witt Jr. there in 1770. She named her first son Dannett Abney Witt, further establishing the connection to the Dannett Abney family line.

The lineage of this family can be traced back to 400 A.D. in England. Their connections to English royalty are well documented, but they were not of royal blood.

William Johnston Father of Martin Johnston; sixth great-grandfather of Jo
Born: 1727, Culpeper County, Virginia
Died: 9 September 1765 in Culpeper County, Virginia
Married: 1752 to Sarah McClaren
Buried: Probably in Culpeper County, Virginia

What little we know of William is from his will and estate papers of 1765, in which he names his wife and children. He spent his life in Culpeper County and died at the age of thirty-eight. His children were:
- Elizabeth Guthrie 1756–1825
- George 1756–1841. Served in the same unit as brother Martin
- Martin 1758–1820. Emma Jo's fifth great-grandfather
- Jean Bloys 1760–1850
- Leanah 1762–?

Jacob Oglesby Sr. Father of Jacob Oglesby Jr.; Emma Jo's sixth great-grandfather
Born: 1709, Henrico County, Virginia
Died: 1780 in Amherst County, Virginia
Married: 1726 in Goochland County, Virginia, to Constance Perkins (1709–1769)
Buried: Unknown location

Jacob Sr. is the son of Richard (Ogilvie) Oglesby (1688–1731) and Susanna Ware of Goochland County, Virginia. His father was born in Angus, Scotland. The name Oglesby is derived from the Scotch name of Ogilvie, and we can trace this line to the eleventh century in Scotland. Jacob was born in Henrico County but grew up in Goochland County, where his father owned a plantation.

He married Constance Perkins in 1726. As was discussed above, her last name is in question as their marriage records do not show her last name. Some researchers attribute her last name of Perkins to the fact that her father, Nicholas Perkins, was a neighboring land owner to his father. We have also seen records that show her middle name as Christian.

Jacob was a farmer in Goochland County as we found records of neighbors who owned adjacent land, but we do not know the amount of land he owned. We doubt if he owned slaves. Jacob and Constance had the following children:

- William 1727–1802
- Richard 1729–1799
- Thomas 1735–1799
- Jacob Jr. 1736–1813
- Nancy Anna 1738–1830
- David 1740–1821

Chapter 11
Ninth Generation—Seventh Great-Grandparents

"You live as long as you are remembered."

– Russian Proberb

Pilgrim John William Guillaume Witt Father of David Witt Sr.; Jo's seventh great-grandfather
Born: 1675 in Pays D'Aunis Laroc, France
Died: 1754 in Albemarle County, Virginia
Married: 1696 in England and again in Albemarle County, Virginia, in 1705 to Elizabeth
Mildred Daux
Buried: Unknown location probably near Charlottesville

In 1696 John William—as a member of the Huguenots who recently fled France—departed Southampton, England, for America. They were fleeing from King Louis XIV of France, who was not fond of non-Catholic Frenchmen. The English king was quick to award land grants in the colony of Virginia and have them gone. They were led by Marquis Oliver de la Muce. When they arrived in Virginia, they formed the colony of Manakin in what later became Powhatan County. William's full last name of Guillaume was not used in the colonies, but the name of Witt was retained.

William married Elizabeth Daux before leaving England and again in Albemarle County. Their children were born in Virginia.

The grants given to William around 1701 were located in what was then Henrico Shire, which was later divided into Goochland, Albemarle, and Amherst Counties, parts of which are now Nelson County, Virginia. He bought, sold, and traded land on numerous occasions, and those records remain, documenting much of his family and business contacts. As mentioned earlier in this book, his son David Sr. obtained land grants in Henry County in southern Virginia and signed an oath of allegiance there in 1777. His grandson David Jr. inherited much of his grandfather's land in present-day Nelson County. David Jr.'s daughter Celia married Jesse Oglesby, and their daughter Maria "Mary" married Ellis Roney, and their daughter Elizabeth married Fielding Murphy, Emma Jo's great-grandfather.

William left a will in 1754 in which he did not name all his children, but the family is well documented in history. William is recognized as one of the original "Pilgrims" in America. The National Society of Sons and Daughters of Pilgrims has excellent documentation on this family. "My Virginia Kin" database of Provo, Utah—which is based on a publication of the same name published by Strawberry Point Press in 1958—also gives a genealogy of this family. The names of his sons were obtained from the Pilgrims Society and the *My Virginia Kin* book. The daughters were not mentioned in these sources.

William and Elizabeth Mildred's known children were:
- John 1710–1782. Served in the Revolutionary War
- Benjamin 1712–1770. Served in the Virginia House of Burgess
- Charles 1712–1781. Served in the Revolutionary War
- David Sr. 1720–1808. Jo's sixth great-grandfather, performed patriotic service
- Lewis 1722–1774
- Abner 1725–1756
- Agnes Key 1731–1788. Named in his will
- Sarah Canidey Unknown dates. Named in his will

All of his sons that lived long enough either served in the Revolutionary War or are recognized as a Patriot for service. We were uncertain if William was a slaveholder until we located his will. As with son David and grandson David Jr., he left a slave to his daughter Sarah. Actually, the slave was loaned to her until her husband decided to return and live with her. At that point, the slave was to be divided among the remainder of his children. I suppose the slave would have been unhappy to see Sarah's husband John return. Son Benjamin was the executor of his will, so perhaps he would have been responsible for dividing the slave into equal parts.

Captain Thomas Edward Ashby Sr. Father of the Ashby clan of Patriots; Emma Jo's seventh great-grandfather
Born: October 1682 in Leicestershire, England
Died: 4 August 1752, Shenandoah Valley, Clarke County, Virginia
Married: 1700 in Stafford County, Virginia, to Rosanna "Rose" Berry
Buried: Unknown location

Thomas is the elder member of the American Ashby family. He is son of John Ashby and Elizabeth Thorogood of England. We believe he arrived in Virginia around 1690. As was discussed earlier in the book, we have extensively researched this family line and devoted a chapter in our *Patriots* book to this line from Captain Thomas Sr. to General Turner Ashby of the Civil War. They made history and left their mark on the state of Virginia. We will not recount these stories here, but this is an interesting family in many ways. He and Rosanna had ten children:
- John 1707–1797. Patriot
- Benjamin 1708–1804. Patriot

- Robert 1710–1792. Patriot
- Thomas Jr. 1714–1883. Patriot
- Elizabeth Hardin 1723–1758
- Rose Timmons 1724–1758
- Henry 1725–1798. Patriot
- Stephen 1727–1797. Patriot
- Sarah Byrum 1729–1752
- Ann 1733–1752

All his sons, most grandsons, and several great-grandsons were also Patriots. Some gave their lives.

One merely needs to drive U.S. Route 50 across the Ashby Gap in Clarke County and see the historical marker road signs to begin the study of this family. Other landmarks mentioning members of this family abound across the state.

George Abney Father of Dannett Abney III above; Emma Jo's seventh great-grandfather
Born: 1697 in Gloucester County, Virginia
Died: 1 October 1766 in Halifax County, Virginia
Married: 1728 in Halifax County to Unity Meredith
Buried: St. John's Episcopal Church Cemetery in Halifax County

George is the son of Dannett Abney II of Halifax County, Virginia, and an unknown mother. We would like to point out that the given name of Dannett skipped the George Abney generation, but the number suffix continued with Dannett III discussed in the earlier chapter.

George and Unity owned at least one thousand acres of Virginia farmland in Halifax County. In his will of 13 October 1766 he divided his land among his five named sons. There may have been an unnamed son, but that is uncertain. We found no records of slaves in his will or other records, but given the size of his plantation, we should assume there were slaves and that they were already in the possession of his sons, but that is speculation. He named no daughters in his will, but we believe there was at least one daughter. His children were:
- Dannett III 1730–1809. Discussed above
- Dorcus Mays 1732–1804
- Captain Nathaniel 1734–1806. Revolutionary War surgeon
- Michael 1736–1832
- Captain William 1736–1840. Revolutionary War officer

Richard (Ogilvie) Oglesby Father of Jacob Oglesby; Jo's seventh great-grandfather
Born: 31 March 1688 in Newtyle, Angus, Scotland
Died: 15 February 1731, Goochland County, Virginia
Married: 19 September 1707 in Henrico County, Virginia, to Susanna Adams Ware
Buried: Unknown location

Richard was the son of Dr. William (Ogilvie) Oglesby and Isobell Fleming of Goochland County, originally of Angus, Scotland. His father—as were Richard and his son Jacob Sr. and Jacob Jr.—was a tobacco plantation owner in Goochland County in Virginia. We have documented the spelling of Isobell from several official documents.

In 1728, Goochland County was one of the original counties of the Virginia colony. It was formed from the Henrico Shire, and by 1744 Goochland was divided into several new counties. Among the new counties were Amherst, Nelson, and Albemarle, as well as others. We have found records of land ownership, probate, marriage, and other legal actions involving five generations of this family in all of these counties. The original Goochland County stretched on both sides of the James River to the Blue Ridge Mountains. To accurately place a given family, one must first date the transaction and then relate it to the map in existence at that time. As we developed the stories of the Oglesby family from Dr. William Oglesby (tenth generation) through the generations to Jesse Oglesby (sixth generation), we have strived to place them in the county or counties as those locations existed at that time. In reality, they never wandered far from their roots near present-day Richmond.

Chapter 12
Hawkins Cemetery

"It is a desirable thing to be well-descended, but the glory belongs to our ancestors."

—Plutarch

Our extensive research of the Painter/Scott lines has drawn attention to a Monroe County cemetery in which a number of family members are buried. Our search yielded the following list of names, some with stone markers and some not. We felt this list would be useful for future generations, even though most of these ancestors are not fully documented as being buried there. We discussed our reasons for believing these family members are buried here earlier in the book. I have located numerous unmarked grave spots outside the back fence of the cemetery and strongly believe some, if not all, of the unmarked graves are located there. Note: I have a proven track record of locating unmarked graves. We hope this effort will serve as a memorial of these family members. It is part of the story.

Name	Relationship	Stone Found
John Thomas Painter	Great-Grandfather	No
Margaret "Maggie" Carman*	Great-Grandmother	No
Isaac Painter	Grand Uncle	No
Mason Painter	Grand Uncle	No
Fred Painter	Grand Uncle	No
Mary Elizabeth Painter*	Grand Aunt	No
John M. Amos Painter	Second Great-Grandfather	No
James Henry B. Carman	Second Great-Grandfather	Yes
Mary Ann Schulse	Second Great-Grandmother	Yes
James Edward Carman	Great-Grand Uncle	No
George H. P. Painter	Great-Grand Uncle	Yes
Grace Bee Painter	Aunt, Oliver's Sister	No

*Both Maggie Painter and her daughter Mary Elizabeth are certainly buried there as their death certificates seem to prove this.

In addition to the abovenamed Carmans, there are seven others from this family with marked graves in this cemetery. We did not list them here.

Hawkins Cemetery is located about three miles west of State Route 107 on State Route U on the south side of the road across from the Cannon Lake water tower. It is located on private property, and permission is needed to gain access. It is a well-kept cemetery and overlooks Mark Twain Lake.

This cemetery was first established by the Morton family and was first used by that family around 1853–54. It was sometimes referred to as Harmony Cemetery as the Harmony Baptist Church was located across the road from the cemetery, and it was used by some members of the church. Some death records use that name. It was later referred to as Hawkins Cemetery as it was adjacent to land owned by the Hawkins family. It was also adjacent to land owned by Robert Parker Painter, discussed earlier in this book. The land was probably never deeded as the Hawkins Cemetery, and Monroe County land records show it as a family cemetery, and it is owned by the current owner of the surrounding land. We have copies of these land records.

The Monroe County Historical Society has historical records of the cemetery as well as a list of people buried there with the exception of the above names listed with no tombstones found. It does reflect the names of Maggie and Elizabeth Carman, as their death certificates have been presented for their records.

We should note that the Monroe County Historical Society has published very complete cemetery records of most of the cemeteries in the county. These are published in book form and as CD-ROMs. These records were very useful in our research.

Chapter 13
Final Footprints

"Do not forget the things your eyes have seen or let them slip from your heart as long as you live. Teach them to your children and your children's children."

—Deuteronomy 4:9

Maybe you have not kept count of the ancestors we have presented in this tree, and that is understandable. Of the possible minimum of 128 total ancestors to consider from the first six generations, we have presented the stories of more than 100. Of those 128 possible ancestors, at least 14 were born and probably died in Europe, and it was not our intent to present those stories in this project. We missed a few, and we will continue to search for those missing family members and their stories. We have actually given a glimpse of the seventh and eighth generations, and our research continues much further back, and those stories continue to be developed.

The process we have undergone to uncover these stories—some brief, some intriguing—has pointed to a couple of simple facts. Life is short, and some people leave more footprints to investigate and learn from. The fact that an ancestor left few footprints, or that they are difficult to uncover, should not deter us from the task, for after all, they were worth knowing. They all had stories to tell.

My great-uncle, Bob Younger, was an accomplished researcher, author, and publisher who once told me: "Sonny, my ancestors talk to me." I failed to fully grasp the true meaning of what he had told me. It actually made me feel a little uncomfortable. Now I realize these people do and should talk to us if we listen. There is much to be told and many lessons to be learned.

Even though we have been genealogy researchers for many years, we were stifled by the lack of records available for several Painter family groups. Some of their family groups generated a rich trove of records while some seemed to evaporate into history with few records. Why was that? It became evident that we should not have been so surprised: as has been the case throughout history, disaster strikes. In these instances it was disease, war, and inadequate or lack of medical care. We observed several deaths in the Painter line in Monroe County in 1853. Some of the victims were quite elderly, age sixty-three for example, and some were very young. Diphtheria raged in Monroe County in 1853. We believe this accounted for several Painter family deaths that year. Tuberculosis was also a major killer throughout the nineteenth century. We saw the John Thomas Painter family struck and nearly wiped out by it. The Civil War took its toll on that family also. The result was that wives were left to raise children and pay debts. Some were more successful than others. Sons were left with no land nor the ability to buy land. Family members were buried in unmarked graves. Men who died early and unexpectedly often died intestate. This forced sale of possessions included food, tools, and livestock. The family unit was destroyed. Medical care was clearly lacking in Monroe County. Paris probably had one or more doctors, but ten miles of mud road might as well have been one hundred. Several men and women died way too early, as did infants. We saw examples of more than 50 percent of the children not reaching adulthood in some family groups.

Here are some general observations we gleaned from study of these ancestors:

- We discovered no royalty.
- Most were involved in agriculture in some form. But that was true of most Americans of past eras.
- There were no politicians except maybe one Painter fourth great-uncle.
- We found no exceptionally wealthy relatives.
- There were few college graduates. In fact, many could not read or write well or at all.
- We failed to discover any relative spending time in jail, except POWs. That striped outerwear in the photo above may be an exception.
- The westward population movement of the nineteenth century was central to nearly every family presented.
- They valued basic freedoms: religion, speech, association, and land ownership. They fought for those freedoms and fought hard.

We discovered an interesting fact about the Painter-Scott lines early in our research for the *Patriots* book. We believe nearly all the lines we have studied were present in colonial America prior to the revolution. Several great-grandfathers immigrated and quickly took up arms to defend their new freedoms in the Revolutionary War. Others had been here a long while before the revolution. We can trace one line to Jamestown.

All the lines have western-European roots: England, Scotland, Ireland, France, and Germany. We were unable to trace the Scott family line to the shores, but the name gives that one away. That line was present for the revolution, of that we are confident.

Acknowledgments

Production of this book exploring the Painter and Scott family lines of Missouri would not have been successful without the information and assistance provided by several individuals and organizations. We want to recognize and thank them in a heart-felt way.

These stories and family history information has been gleaned from many sources and presented in a manner we hope readers will find both interesting and informative. We have relied on family bibles, family stories, and handwritten records of the late Richard Scott and Lou Bridgford Callis. Their work from many years ago helped us expand our knowledge of the Scott and Murphy families.

We relied heavily on court, tax, property, and marriage records from the seven states these families lived in or passed through on their migration to the state of Missouri. These are footprints I believe they were unaware of being left for us as they moved westward.

Much of our research of the Revolutionary War Patriots featured in this book was centered on the fact that several of them were recognized by descendants as they documented this service for their membership in the Daughters of the American Revolution (DAR) or the Sons of the American Revolution (SAR). Those records were useful in our quest for resources supporting that service. We hope that in the future, other descendants will find our records useful in their quest for membership in either of these great organizations.

We want to thank the Monroe County Missouri Historical Society for the assistance given in research of several cemeteries in Monroe County, and in particular, the Hawkins cemetery.

The National Archives Census reports and military records were essential in documenting the everyday lives and contributions these families made to this great country.

www.ingramcontent.com/pod-product-compliance
Lightning Source LLC
Chambersburg PA
CBHW050619110426
42813CB00010B/2615